*You may promise yourself every thing — but health,
without which there is no happiness. An attention to health
then should take the place of every other object.*

•

Thomas Jefferson, 1787

Also by Melvin Konner

•

The Tangled Wing

Becoming a Doctor

The Paleolithic Prescription
(with S. Boyd Eaton and Marjorie Shostak)

Why the Reckless Survive and Other Secrets of Human Nature

Childhood

Medicine at the Crossroads

Dear America,

A Concerned Doctor Wants You to Know the Truth About Health Reform

Melvin Konner, M.D.

Addison-Wesley Publishing Company

Reading, Massachusetts • Menlo Park, California • New York
Don Mills, Ontario • Wokingham, England • Amsterdam • Bonn
Sydney • Singapore • Tokyo • Madrid • San Juan
Paris • Seoul • Milan • Mexico City • Taipei

•

To all who are waiting
in the emergency rooms of America,
wondering when someone will take care of them;

and to the brave and good women and men
who, with their own two hands, are trying,
against all odds, to do just that.

•

Library of Congress Cataloging-in-Publication Data

Konner, Melvin.
    Dear America: a concerned doctor wants you to know the truth
about health reform / Melvin Konner.
        p.   cm.
    Includes bibliographical references.
    ISBN 0-201-40631-4
    1. Insurance, Health—Government policy—United States.
2. Medical care. Cost of—United States.   3. Medical Care—United
States—Cost control.   I. Title.
RA395.A3K659   1993
338.4'33621'0973—dc20   93-36625
                                                                          CIP

Cover design by Suzanne Heiser
Production services by Mark Corsey

1 2 3 4 5 6 7 8 9 10-ARM-9796959493
First printing, October 1993

CONTENTS

·

Introduction

DEAR AMERICA,

This open letter is an unabashed brief on behalf of the simplest, best, and most cost-effective approach to health care reform: the single payer option. Although the White House rejects this idea out of hand, it is an idea whose time has come. It is supported by a large and rapidly growing body of Americans, including the leading consumer and labor organizations, six senators, eighty-nine congressional representatives, thousands of doctors, and some leading medical journals and general periodicals. Most important, the majority of Americans polled say they would like a health care system resembling Canada's, which is a single payer system. This support is swelling constantly.

I felt compelled to write for two reasons. First, I write because what is clearly and increasingly the will of the American people is being ignored, in fact trounced on, by a White House and a Congress in the grip of powerful special interests, especially the largest insurance companies—Prudential, Aetna, Cigna, Travelers, and Metropolitan Life—which stand to profit enormously from the Clinton plan announced in September 1993. The Clintons deserve praise for bringing health care into the forefront of America's consciousness for the first time in many years. But their specific plan takes the wrong direction. I could not sit by and watch while ordinary Americans lose a battle they have every right to win. The prize is our free choice of a doctor, and a potential saving of some $100 billion a year that, if we lose, will be dumped into corporate coffers.

Second, ignorance about what is happening, and what is likely to happen, is so widespread that it seemed to me essential to put the facts together in a short, readable form that may be of use to those who are confused as well as to those who are trying to tell the truth amid the cacophony of lies that characterize this debate. The White House and the health-for-profits lobbyists are conducting a truly reprehensible disinformation campaign to discredit single payer, which is clearly the best plan for average Americans—in fact, for every American. The initial reaction to the Clinton plan was a warm one. But the plan is going to be a hard sell, and my advice in this book is, Don't buy.

I am not a health economist or a management analyst, a politician or even a practicing physician. But I do have some credentials.

First, I hold an M.D. degree, and to get it I had to train in clinical settings for two years. I know what it is like to try to help those who are under assault by disease, and unlike so many in the health reform debate, I thoroughly understand the science of disease and its treatments. I have kept abreast of the situations doctors find themselves in by tagging along with them as they discharge their clinical duties. Yet I am not one of them. I do not provide care for patients except occasionally and very informally, and I do not earn any portion of my income by doing so. I personally stand to gain in no way—except as a citizen—from any particular approach to health reform.

Second, both before and since going to medical school, I have been a card-carrying anthropologist—a career that has included two years in the African bush, twenty years teaching premedical students and graduate students interested in health, and several previous books relating to medical and health issues. Unlike most medical school graduates, I see illness and health care in a broad social and cultural context. I understand human inertia as an obstacle to change. But unlike most social scientists, including all those prominent in the health care reform debate so far, I have been to medical school.

Third, like many Americans, I have been personally educated in the school of illness. Since 1987 I have been involved in the care and rehabilitation of a sister-in-law who had a devastating stroke at age forty-three; a wife struggling with cancer; a 4-year-old daughter hospitalized and operated on for snake bite; a father battling multiple illnesses, including heart disease and bladder cancer; and a mother who died after three painful months in the wake of a stroke that robbed her of most of what makes life worthwhile. I myself have been luckier, but I have had major surgery for two ruptured disks in my lower back, and have spent months bedridden over the years in connection with this very painful illness. But although I know firsthand what the threat of illness means, other people and other families have suffered worse, to be sure. For one thing, my family has never had to worry about where the money for treatment would come from. I have spent as many nights in hospitals as a patient or a family member as I did as a medical student.

Fourth, I sit on a committee at my university charged with overseeing a major transition in health care delivery systems. Over the past two years we have gone from a fee-for-service model of care using fully independent physicians and funded by Blue Cross/Blue Shield, to a combined health maintenance organization (HMO)/preferred provider model. This is just the type of change that would be almost universal under the plan the Clintons have introduced. I have heard the bitter complaints of the faculty and staff of the university, seen their choices steadily and unpredictably narrowed, and watched their disappointment as they were forced to give up doctors and other caregivers they had known and trusted for years—even decades. I have transmitted these complaints to the representatives of the for-profit insurance corporation in question, and I have heard their answers. I was not satisfied. I do not relish the thought that these representatives, and others like them, may soon become far more powerful under the half-baked plan cooked up at the White House.

The Clintons have their hearts, but not their minds, in the right place. Their plan, as announced in September 1993, has a host of flaws, but two of them will probably be fatal politically.

The Clinton plan will drastically and relentlessly narrow the individual's choice of caregiver—whether a doctor, a dentist, a psychotherapist, or a nurse practitioner. No one disputes this. Senator

Bob Kerrey of Nebraska, who should know better, recently said that he thought the American people don't care very much about choice of doctor. Polls have already proven him wrong, and the debate over the Clinton plan will make clear just how much Americans do care about choice. But it is not just a question of freedom. I understand the realities of illness and medicine fairly well, and I believe that choice of caregivers is a cornerstone of a properly functioning health care system.

The Clinton plan's other potentially fatal flaw is that it will add a new burden of taxes. The furor over a modest increase in the gasoline tax and some other increases in the 1994 Clinton budget shows how Americans will react to yet another new tax to finance health care for all. They will see it as another entitlement program designed to help others, not themselves. And such a tax will, in fact, cost the middle class more money—$100 billion more at a minimum, according to the Health Care Financing Administration, the federal government's most experienced agency in the payment of health care.

What most Americans have not yet fully grasped is that the single payer approach—an American variant of the Canadian plan—completely avoids both these fatal flaws. Many Americans still think of Canada's system as socialized medicine, with little choice. That is simply false, and is the product of a systematic smear campaign against the Canadian health care system conducted by corporate health insurers and other special interests trying to hold back change. Britain has socialized medicine, with doctors who work for the government, which is the sole health care provider—although even in Britain choice of doctor is wider than it will be in the U.S. under the Clinton plan. But in Canada, only payment—insurance—is government-managed. Doctors are independent. And as a patient you are free to choose from the entire physician corps of the nation.

But what about taxes? Surely taking over the health insurance process will require huge new taxes? Under the Clinton plan, yes. But under a single payer system, only in a technical and trivial sense. Americans are already paying huge sums of money, totaling a seventh of the gross domestic product, to cover the costs of health care. Laws mandate health insurance in many sectors of the economy, and we are taxed, through premiums, by private, for-profit corporations—the major insurance companies—that serve no function in the system except to move money around and cream huge profits off the top. In a single payer system, those wasteful bureaucracies would be gone. Nominally, taxes would increase, but in reality this would be only a shift in the destination of the same payroll deduction. Your premium would be paid to the statewide single payer instead of to the major insurance companies. And the great question of new money to cover the uninsured would simply disappear, as the tremendous bureaucratic waste caused by for-profit insurers shifted into the column of real health care delivered to real people.

Managed competition, the Clintons' completely theoretical approach to cost control, would, on the other hand, cost a fortune to implement, and would provide a whole new layer of bureaucracy. Its final details await congressional debate. Since the inauguration, a coy journalistic cat-and-mouse game has given us glimpses of a confused and clumsy process in which academic abstractions and cynical political ploys vie with each other for prominence. Mr. Clinton's first health care speech as president, addressed to the governors in August 1993, was vague and deliberately misleading. He mocked the Canadian option, claiming that it "would require us to replace over $500 billion in private insurance premiums with nearly that much in new taxes." He knows this is false. That money would simply be shifted from the private insurance premium deduction on our paychecks to an equal or lower deduction paid into a statewide fund, managed by a single state-government-appointed agency. The only difference is that the $500 billion would go entirely for health care instead of first being subject to an insurance-company-profits "tax." Mr. Clinton's own plan, unveiled in September, *does* require a large increase in real taxes. It would harass doctors more than ever, destroy many thousands of small businesses, take away our free choice of doctor, and perpetuate the employer's unfair power over the health of employees. It reflects the undue influence of insurance company magnates more than any other single force. Yet we have felt compelled to take this process seriously as the only health reform game in town.

With peace breaking out in the Middle East, and a warm public reaction to his health plan, President Clinton is no longer at a low ebb of prestige. But the current enthusiasm may pass. He is still bloodied from one-vote majorities on a watered-down budget plan, red-faced over blunders on gays and married couples in the military, and weak on foreign policy and trade. He faces major Republican electoral victories in 1993 in Texas, Los Angeles, and even Arkansas, and powerful lobbyists who are poised to cut the heart out of health reform, as well as a vigorous congressional opposition that is scrapping for any sort of fight. With all this, the Clinton plan is not only *not* the only game in town, it is quite possibly a nonstarter.

I therefore write not as if we need to be grateful for any scraps of reform the government deigns to toss us, nor in an effort to rush to a compromise by Christmas, or spring of 1994, or however it is they are now marking their calendars. I speak instead on behalf of real health reform, on the assumption that what we care about is not the quickest politically feasible compromise, but the best health care system for this nation.

Where managed competition will herd us all into a maze of health maintenance organizations (HMOs) and preferred provider organizations (PPOs), relentlessly narrowing our choices among doctors and other caregivers, the single payer solution leaves our choices completely open. Where managed competition preserves the link between employment and health coverage—a corroded historical relic, disastrous in every way—the single payer solution breaks that link forever. Where managed competition will generate at least $100 billion in new tax burdens for Americans, single payer will add no new costs, only shift them. Where managed competition struggles to preserve a role for the vast commercial bureaucracy that generates a quarter of our health care costs, single payer centralizes the process of payment in state capitals, achieving a far more efficient result at a fraction of the cost. Where managed competition adds a new layer of bureaucracy, the National Health Board, with the long arm of Washington guiding for-profit bureaucracies to control doctors and patients, single payer respects the Constitution by respecting states' rights, and leaves doctors and patients far more freedom.

Most important, however, is the fact that managed competition has never been tried anywhere. It is an incredibly complex blueprint for an imaginary social machine that all of us will have to live in, permanently. It exists only as an abstraction in the minds of a handful of would-be social engineers. Its implementation would be an uncontrolled experiment on the health, wealth, and welfare of the American people. It might work, of course, but there is no practical reason to believe that it would. It is nothing but a castle in the air, and it doesn't look a bit like any castle anyone has seen on solid ground.

Single payer, by contrast, has been tried and has succeeded just north of the border in a culture very much like ours. Ninety-seven percent of Canadians say in polls that they like their system. Border crossing, contrary to what you have heard, is minimal. Today, Canadians spend about a third less money per person per year on health care than we do, yet have much better infant mortality and longevity statistics. Even doctors, who earn about two-thirds as much as doctors in the United States but have no administrative hassles, are relatively satisfied. Other advanced industrial nations have health care delivery systems that resemble single payer far more than they do managed competition. The experiment has been done. Single payer works. Obviously, the giant insurance companies do not want you to know these simple facts, because in Canada the people decided to put those companies out of the health business.

If you doubt what I say, ask yourself (and your congressional representative) these questions:

- Why does the government consistently lie about health and medicine in Canada?

- Why has the White House tried so hard to suppress all debate about the single payer option?

- Who gave six or eight insurance business giants a death grip on the process of health reform?

- Who will be doing the managing in managed competition?

- Why is it all right to close military bases and lay off people who have served their country for years, but not to downsize useless health insurance firms like Aetna, Prudential, and Travelers?

- Why must America, the last industrialized country to look seriously at health reform, be offered an academic fairy tale—managed competition—that has never been tried anywhere, while our leaders ignore proven plans that have worked well abroad?

- Why does the government want to take away our free choice of doctor, while our friends north of the border keep their freedom of choice?

- Why does small business have to pay such a heavy price, while big business reaps all the benefits?

- And why does the White House want to delay universal coverage for seven or more years when every civilized country already has it?

You don't have to be poor to love the single payer approach. You just have to want good care at reasonable prices. You have to care about your own choice of doctor. You have to want to avoid overtreatment as well as undertreatment. You have to be willing to sacrifice thousands of unproductive jobs in the insurance business in order to produce thousands of productive jobs for nurses, therapists, and other health professionals. You don't even have to care about the uninsured—not even to the extent that you would rather avoid having their abandonment nagging at your conscience. You just have to think it would be more sensible to pay a smaller amount for timely care of this group than a large amount for care that is too little too late.

Hardheaded as I like to be, however, I must admit that the uninsured have nagged at my conscience—ever since I first saw their faces, as they sat bleeding or burning with fever, scared half to death or bent over in pain, hour after hour, in the emergency ward waiting areas of the great and famous hospitals where I had my medical school clerkships. They, and the other Americans who are joining their ranks daily as we lose our health care coverage, have a permanent claim on my consciousness. Their illnesses can often be prevented with timely care, care that they cannot now get, even though such care would save the system money. The great theologian Reinhold Niebuhr used to say that our job in this life is to comfort the afflicted and afflict the comfortable. To my friends and colleagues in medicine, who trained so long, work so hard, do so much good for so many, and have taught me so much: Please don't overlook my respect for you in what follows. I don't want to seem disloyal, and I do value your friendship. But I keep being haunted by those faces.

THE

CRISIS

WHAT HAS HAPPENED to American medicine's Golden Age?

Just a couple of decades ago it seemed that doctors could do no wrong. Medical miracles lay like jewels to be picked up each time we turned a corner. Penicillin, streptomycin, cortisone, polio vaccine, open-heart surgery, the heart-lung machine, psychiatric drugs, kidney dialysis, transplants—three decades ago there seemed to be no end to what we could do, and no limit to medicine's confidence. America clearly did have the best health care in the world, and it seemed sure only to get better.

Yet today there is widespread agreement that the system is not working. Thirty-seven million uninsured Americans cannot pay for health care, and that alarming number is constantly growing. The underinsured are more difficult to count, but are at least as numerous as the uninsured. In addition, cost control is on everyone's mind, since it is not difficult to figure out that surging costs are the riptide swelling the ranks of the uninsured. Any average American may eventually be engulfed. Medical catastrophe, job loss, insurance company scams, or just a continuing anemia of the economy could bring the disaster of medical abandonment home to any one of us, or our children.

These issues are of tremendous importance, and are popular subjects for discussion and analysis. But there are also other fundamental and pervasive problems in our nation's health care system, and it is very unlikely that reform will work without addressing them.

• Trust between doctor and patient has broken down on both sides. Increasingly cold and transient encounters characterize what was once called healing. Medical gurus like Bernie Siegel, a former cancer surgeon who promotes mind-over-illness healing, fill large auditoriums with seriously ill people who are deeply dissatisfied with their doctors, and they deliberately incite their audiences to rebel. "Get angry at your doctor," urges Siegel, and people do. Doctors turn out to be a very easy target. Some of them are selfish, but many more are just awkward socially and don't have the time to build a good doctor-patient alliance. Millions of people go to quacks just for a kind word. It is estimated that the amount Americans now spend for "alternative healing" is about equal to the amount we spend on mainstream medicine. People resent what they perceive as doctors' inflated incomes. And, of course, we sue at the drop of a stethoscope. There is an enormous well of anger out there against doctors, and it is helping to fuel a hasty and ill-conceived process of health reform.

• Grotesque imbalances tilt medicine away from primary care and prevention and weigh heavily against needed public health measures. Dubious high-tech procedures displace proven tactics any family physician or nurse practitioner can perform. Only 30 percent of America's physician corps is on the front lines, in primary care, as against 50 percent or more in Canada and England. In last year's U.S. medical school graduating class, only 15 percent chose primary care specialties. That means that at a time when we desperately need more primary care doctors, we are going to have fewer every year for the foreseeable future. This is because reimbursement patterns are ludicrous. Insurers pay for procedures, not for time; but the currency of primary care *is* time. It is the time spent taking the patient's history, the most vital and informative part of the doctor-patient encounter. It is the time spent explaining how to take the medicine, what to eat, how to exercise. Above all, it is the time spent creating a therapeutic alliance, a collaborative trust, a collegial bond between the doctor and the patient that is absolutely essential to any process of healing. Yet, ignoring all this, we consistently reimburse procedures rather than time, creating a system top-heavy with technology and impoverishing primary care doctors while enriching knife- and laser-happy surgeons.

Surgeons earn five to ten times as much as their primary care colleagues. Which would you choose to be, if you were a medical student?

• Doctors live in fear of litigation and defensively drive costs up, trying to leave no scan unturned. Yet litigation, for which we all pay (and far more than its direct costs), compensates few of the wronged patients and punishes few of the bad doctors. A 1991 study in New York State led by Russell Localio, an attorney and public health expert, reviewed over 31,000 hospital records. It found that about 1 percent of patients clearly had legitimate claims to compensation. Yet under 2 percent of these patients even filed a claim, which is only a first, chancy step toward compensation. It is estimated that only half of these filers, or under 1 percent of all patients injured by negligence, will achieve settlements. Ironically, more than half of the cases actually brought by patients were *not* in the category independently judged to merit compensation.

Because of the large size of some of these awards—up to millions of dollars—there is a widespread impression that this is a good way of controlling physician error. It is not. The vast majority of truly negligent acts by U.S. doctors are not detected and certainly not punished. This is not true elsewhere. In Sweden, to take one example, the mechanism for compensating patients who experience losses due to doctor error is separate from the one for punishing and restricting bad doctors. This allows doctors actually to help patients recover their compensation, independent of the courts. The awards are much smaller—tens to hundreds of thousands of dollars—but a far higher percentage of patients are compensated. Yet ironically, in the U.S., the fear of being ruined by a lawsuit is so frightening to doctors that they practice intensely defensive medicine. A large factor in what they decide to do with patients—tests, procedures, and the like—is the fear of litigation. Some official estimates of the total cost of medical litigation, including defensive medicine, range up to the tens of billions of dollars annually. But it is very difficult to estimate this cost,

and the total bill for medical lawsuits may be much higher. As with the
S & L debacle, officially claimed losses are probably only a fraction of
real cost.

• Overtreatment of the insured is every bit as rife in our system as
undertreatment of the uninsured, and it results in needless cost,
discomfort, illness, and death. Experts bicker about whether the Food
and Drug Administration moves too slowly or too quickly in the
approval of new drugs. Yet surgical and diagnostic procedures are
implemented and paid for in the billions year after year with no such
scrutiny at all. Coronary bypasses, angiograms, angioplasties, pacemaker implantations, cesarean sections, hysterectomies, prostate operations, and other invasive procedures are done thousands of times a
year more often than they are indicated. That is, not only are they
unnecessary in retrospect—Monday morning quarterbacking is no
great trick—but they could have been judged in advance, on accepted
criteria, to have been unnecessary. Yet they are done, and approved,
and paid for, in enormous excess, again and again and again.

• People who cannot afford insurance premiums do not get health
care unless they are poor enough to get Medicaid or old enough to get
Medicare. This is the well known uninsured population. Eighty-five
percent of them are working—in agriculture, building trades, service
industries, and other productive areas of our economy. But there are
others who work, earn substantial incomes, and can afford insurance,
yet cannot get it because they are uninsurable. This may be because
the person or a spouse or child is already ill, or it may just mean that
the person is at higher-than-average risk: a parent died young of a
heart attack or breast cancer, or the person himself is a male hairdresser
or flight attendant, an occupational category that is at higher risk for
AIDS. These sickening practices, known as "cherry picking" or
"redlining," are simply not permitted in any other civilized country.
When these people show up at the emergency room door, the care
they get is too little too late, yet it costs far more than it would have
cost to care for them in a rational, timely way.

• We tie health insurance to employment, a disastrous choice in every way. It keeps people in jobs they detest ("job lock"), tosses them off the health coverage rolls as soon as they are laid off, and gives managers the most unfair sort of leverage over their employees. Millions of people are afraid to change jobs, fearing that they may lose their coverage. Some people are simply dropped from insurance plans when they get sick, after an absurdly low, newly invoked maximum payment. Others who become ill while insured may find that the company raises premiums, say, tenfold one year, and then gives 90 percent discounts to the employees who are not yet sick. This practice, "policy churning," is not just cherry picking, it is cherry picking after the facts of coverage and illness both, and it renders insurance no more than a con game, a scam.

• Most inexcusable of all, perhaps, we shovel a fifth of our precious health care dollars into the administrative furnaces of commercial insurance companies, a vast, parasitic bureaucracy that is completely unresponsive to the needs of the nation. Insurance company bean counters and health care "providers"—a detestable and deliberately denigrating word for caregivers—dance around each other in a macabre minuet that saps the spirit of those who give care.

Administrators in the health care system have multiplied like rabbits. Since 1970, the number of administrators in health care has increased *four times as fast* as the number of doctors, which has crept up very slowly. Although these administrators claim that their harassment of doctors controls costs, the fact is the enormous rise in health care costs is virtually superimposable on the enormous rise in the number of administrators. No economist can measure the cost of this harassment in the morale of physicians and other caregivers, but the cost is unquestionably very high, and so too are the attendant risks. Because the caregiver without morale is likely sooner or later to become a caregiver without morals. It is a small step from resenting society to resenting patients, and I for one do not relish the prospect of putting my life in the hands of a person who resents me. Harassment of physicians is a no-win proposition, regardless of what health care system we have, and we continue to harass doctors at our peril.

The crisis we are facing is in no way a monopoly of the poor. It affects all sectors of society, and everyone is afraid that its effects will soon be apparent in their lives, if they aren't already. Even though the roaring eighties are over, selfishness once again rather in bad taste, and a sense of national community again somewhat on the rise, concern for the poor is not the main driving force in health reform. Concern for ourselves is. And that is legitimate, since, even if we want to help those coming up behind us, we have to be sure of our own health to do anyone else any good. And we are less sure of it all the time. Because the uninsured and underinsured are no longer just the poor. They are, or soon could be, you and me.

By definition, all are too rich to qualify for Medicaid. According to Families USA, a nonprofit Washington policy group, 2 million people lose their health insurance each month, at least temporarily. Eventually 95 percent of them will regain it, but that still adds 100,000 permanently uninsured to the rolls every thirty days, more than a million a year. Could that million a year include you or me next year, or the year after? Easily.

A sixth of all working people are already in that category, according to the Employee Benefit Research Institute. The job category with the highest proportion of uninsured is farming, at 40 percent. So much for the notion that the problem is centered in inner-city ghettos. Thirty-five percent of people working in personal services, 31 percent of construction workers, and 26 percent of people in business and repair services have no health care coverage. These are productive people, growing things, building, fixing, helping. If they or their children get sick, who will help them? Fully 22 percent of self-employed people are uninsured. What will happen to the American entrepreneurial dream if people are too scared of illness to chance it? Increasingly, it is apparent that such fears weigh heavily in our hearts and on our economy. People in Europe and Japan do not have to deal with such fears. Can we win our economic race with them if we are wearing this extra weight? I seriously doubt it.

Who has calculated the dollar cost of job lock? No one that I have seen, but it must be at least in the scores of billions. *Job lock* means fear of changing jobs when you and your family might be uninsurable in your new job. Is this the open and free market the Republicans and conservative Democrats always go on about? There are probably tens of millions of Americans who could sell their skills and experience on the open market and help get the economy moving by matching their dreams to employers' needs. But they never will, because although their talents and knowledge can go with them, their health insurance can't. Think of these underapplied and misapplied talents as a countable (though uncounted) loss to our nation's economy. It must be massive.

But that's not the worst of it. According to the Department of Health and Human Services, one in four Americans who has insurance today will lose it, at least temporarily, during the next two years. One in four. Of course, if it happens to you, you will probably get it back in a matter of months or years. But what if you or your loved ones get sick in the interim? You could easily become permanently uninsurable.

And what happens then? When you or, say, a child of yours gets sick, you pay out of pocket. A hundred dollars, a thousand, a hundred thousand, whatever it takes. If you are under sixty-five you will not be eligible for public assistance until you are legally impoverished. But this can easily happen to an average middle-class family in a case of major illness. A series of bypass operations, for instance—almost any middle-aged person could need them—might cost as much as $50,000 or $100,000. So you spend yourself into poverty, and then when you have nothing left, you qualify for the second-rate medical care offered you by Medicaid.

But let's say you are lucky enough to stay insured. You're protected, right? Not necessarily. You may not have read the fine print in your company's policy. You may have large co-payments and deductibles, or an absurdly low ceiling of payment. Your insurance company may go broke, or it may engage in one of the various scams that have become common to avoid paying for your care once you become sick.

What scams? Virtually all insurance companies close pools, allowing the healthy to switch to lower-priced pools and leaving the sick behind to face premiums that rise relentlessly in price until they are forced to drop out. This protects the "insurer" from having to do what he promised: care for the pool member who gets sick.

Insurance companies use a loophole in federal law to protect themselves from lawsuits by people they drop from their rolls because of illness. This loophole, part of the Employee Retirement Income Security Act (ERISA) of 1974, makes insurance companies unique among American corporations and individuals by insulating them from liability or even criminal prosecution. They are protected by what is just plain bad law.

The insurance industry has also somehow managed to maintain a long-standing immunity from federal antitrust law. A representative of Consumers Union said in June 1993, "Health insurance companies decide not to provide coverage for people in certain ZIP codes. They decide which diseases will be covered and which ones won't. But these practices are shielded from antitrust scrutiny."

If you are getting nervous about all this, you should be.

Still, maybe you're not the type to worry. Or you have an ironclad insurance policy and 100 percent job security. Plus, you're not the type to shed any tears about the poor. They get enough; let them pull themselves up by their own bootstraps. Why should you support health reform for their sake, or anyone's? Why should you have to pay for their health care?

The simple fact is, you already do.

Unless you are prepared to let the poor die in the streets—and, indeed, to convince the majority of your fellow citizens to be equally detached from their suffering—you will continue to pay for them whenever they show up at the emergency room door. You will pay for them in taxes that cover Medicaid and Medicare. You will pay for them in exaggerated insurance premiums gouged out of your pay-check, so the hospital where you are covered can make ends meet. And you will pay for them in the relentless and devastating inflation that makes health care costs soar in a clear blue sky high above everything else.

You've read about the hospitals that charge five dollars for a Tylenol. Maybe you're even one of those rare insured individuals who actually read the hospital bill, and you've seen it for yourself in black and white. What gives? Some of the charge is "handling": the pharmacist has to dole it out; the administrators have to account for it; the nurse has to come when you call, evaluate your pain, and bring you the pill. But a large part of the five dollars is your or your insurance company's charitable contribution for the care of the uninsured, the ones almost none of us are willing to turn away. The 10-year-old boy with asthma who can't breathe. The lady with the cancer that ruptured her intestine.

If the system were different, you could have paid a little and done them a lot more good. But you would have to agree to pay when they are not in such distress. You would have to be compassionate with your mind as well as your heart. Since most of us aren't, we wait until the worst happens, and then, when we find we can't say no, we dig deep and pay far more.

If you haven't been hospitalized or if you ignored the bill and can't visualize a five-dollar Tylenol, try this: look at the summary of deductions on your paycheck every month. If you are insured, you are paying a premium for the privilege, and that premium is rising rapidly. In all likelihood, you have almost no control over how large that premium gets, how big a bite is taken by the commercial insurance profiteers, or what they will actually do for you or a family member in illness. Faceless bureaucrats get into meetings with your employer and together they decide what is "best." They eat up a big chunk of the health care dollar that in other countries goes directly to care of the sick. And they take your money away—look at the check stub—month after month after month.

For some reason Americans identify the word "bureaucracy" only with government agencies. I know they're out there, and I've dealt with some doozies. But they are not the only bureaucracies or even the largest or clumsiest ones. Health care delivery is a process fatally weighted down by a vast, parasitic, private corporate bureaucracy, backed by an army of hungry stockholders, that taxes you almost as surely as government does, but (believe it or not) wastes far more of your money.

Study after study has demonstrated this waste. Most recently, in the *New England Journal of Medicine* in August 1993, Dr. Steffie Woolhandler and her colleagues at Cambridge City Hospital in Massachusetts showed that our hospital administrative costs amount to 25 percent of every health care dollar. The comparable figure in Canada is 11 percent. The disparity results from U.S. hospitals' need to respond constantly to insurance company demands. You are supporting, through your monthly premium deduction, many thousands of people who do jobs that not only don't need to be done but actually increase the costs and hurt the morale of health care professionals and their patients—us. This is the largest entitlement program in the private sector outside the military–industrial complex. It is nothing but a welfare program for corporate bureaucrats who might otherwise have to seek useful employment. You pay them high salaries, but they don't do anything for you, and you should fire them just as soon as possible.

Yet saying that they don't do anything for you is to understate the case. These people, more than anyone else, are responsible for the grotesque distortions that have become commonplace in our health care system over the past thirty years. Collaborating first with the greediest minority of doctors, and later with corporate owners of hospitals and clinics, they have managed to all but destroy some of the best aspects of the American health care delivery system and to institutionalize some dreadful habits and practices that will be extremely difficult for our country to eliminate. Now they are moving aggressively into managed care itself by buying up many large HMOs.

Corporate power in the illness business is becoming more concentrated by the day, month, and year. The distinction between the insurance racket and HMOs themselves is becoming meaningless. These takeovers will get the government stamp of approval in big red letters if managed competition succeeds. "By any measure, private insurance is big business in America," wrote respected commentator John Inglehart in the June 1992 *New England Journal of Medicine.* He might have added that it is getting bigger by the minute, while our health care system is getting worse.

We used to have, in the United States, a large corps of primary care practitioners, doctors right on the front lines, who knew and were trusted by their patients. Other countries in the industrial West have half or more of their physicians serving in such roles. We have fewer than 30 percent in what is a continuing downward trend. Who has greater longevity and lower infant mortality? The other countries do. Why? Because primary care doctors are the ones who take care of you. They know you and want you to be well. They understand your history, so they know what your symptoms mean—before they order expensive and dangerous tests. It is their goal to help you avoid major medical and surgical procedures that you may not need, but that would profit a specialist if you consulted the specialist first.

We know that the shortage of primary care isn't good for us, and we have known that for more than a quarter century. That is how far back you can find solemn pronouncements from medical educators about stopping the relentless slide away from primary care. Medical schools instituted programs, propaganda, and exhortations to no avail. The slide continued and continues. We have specialists, subspecialists, and sub-subspecialists, more of them every year. An analysis published in 1993 in the journal *Health Affairs* showed that if, starting now, 100 percent of the graduating classes of America's medical schools were to choose primary care as their field, it would be 2004 before half of our doctors were primary care practitioners. If half the graduating class of each chose primary care, it would take until 2040 for the same goal to be reached.

But neither of these scenarios is possible. What percentage of medical graduates in 1992 chose primary care fields? Fifteen. And if past experience is any guide, many of these will change their minds and specialize later. So what will actually happen if current trends continue? We will not even be asking when we can reach the goal of having half the physician work force in primary care. We will be moving in the opposite direction. The proportion of primary care practitioners today—30 percent, considered far too low by leading medical educators and public health authorities—will decline further, reaching 15 percent in less than half a century. And every aspect of our current crisis, including unfairness, neglect, waste, and out-of-control costs, will get worse.

These trends are easy to explain. Medical school graduates are not stupid. They see their teachers in surgical and technology-based specialties reaping incomes consistently over $300,000 a year, with top incomes in the millions. And they see internists, pediatricians, family practitioners, and others in primary care earning less than $100,000—often much less. They see the first group living in the house on the hill, playing golf every Wednesday afternoon, and concerning themselves increasingly with their investments, while the second group spend their lives talking on the phone with insurance company clerks, filling out endless forms, and being unable to afford a nurse or secretary to assist them. Many medical students are idealists: witness the tremendous increase in applications during the last few years, despite confusing winds of change that might blow the big incomes away. But only the most idealistic can be expected to choose primary care when we really give them no choice at all.

What explains this enormous difference in the income and life situations of the two groups of doctors?

Traditionally, before World War II, surgeons were the main specialists. In the 1930s, only 10 percent of doctors were surgeons, and three-fourths were general practitioners. As the insurance companies began to grow in the forties and fifties, they reinforced and then exaggerated the disparity in reimbursement between specialists and primary care doctors. A culture of reimbursement grew up, and became set in stone, which recognized the value of procedures but not of time. At the center of this was the false notion that reimbursement for time is subject to abuse, while reimbursement for procedures is not.

In fact, today the abuse of procedures, and of reimbursement for them—both in terms of the number of needless ones done and in terms of the amount paid for each—is clearly a key factor in our health cost crisis. Overpaid specialists doing too many procedures, in collusion with the insurance companies who shamelessly favored these specialists, have conspired to manipulate millions of patients and to oppress primary care doctors. Today the average primary care office doctor in the state of Vermont makes $55,000 a year, according to Governor Howard Dean, who is an M.D. himself. The average orthopedic surgeon makes well over $200,000. A 1989 study, "Choice in Specialty: It's Money That Matters in the U.S.A.," showed an almost perfect correlation between the income in a specialty and the ease with which it filled its available slots for trainees.

Princeton sociologist Paul Starr has detailed the history of the growth in number of medical specialists beautifully. Surgeons and other specialists took signal advantage of their hospital-based position to band together with hospitals, insurers, and eventually with hospital corporations, to keep their prices and incomes inflated. With the dramatic expansion of medical schools and residency programs during the 1960s, these specialists were able to draw on an army of low-paid residents to take over much of their work. The medical schools and hospitals tried to get the specialists to compensate part of this labor, without success. In the end, the surgeons made ever more money while working fewer hours. Meanwhile, primary care practitioners had to work sixty to eighty hours a week to make ends meet, resulting in an hourly wage no different from that of auto mechanics. They more than doubled the number of patients they saw each day, relentlessly reducing the time they spent with each.

But as Julian Tudor-Hart, a distinguished leader of primary care doctors in Wales, has aptly said, "The currency of primary care is time"—time spent with patients finding out about the symptoms, explaining the options for treatment, describing the needed regimens of medicine, diet, and exercise, and alerting the patient to those changes that should be seen as a warning. An excellent 1975 study showed that more than 85 percent of the information a doctor uses to make a diagnosis comes from the history alone, from talking to the patient about the illness. The diagnosis reached after the history was taken had to be changed after the physical exam in only about 7 percent of cases, and after a battery of tests in only another 7 percent. Studies of compliance with the doctor's recommendations—even at the simplest level, such as taking the pills in the right dosage at the right time—show that it is alarmingly poor, largely because doctors have no time to explain anything, and indeed have no relationship with the patient.

At first glance it would seem to be against the interests of the insurance companies to pay for expensive surgery and other procedures, often of dubious value. So why do they? There are two explanations. First, insurance company bureaucrats are no less susceptible than the rest of us to the illusion that technology is magic and that every problem must have a technical quick fix. Second, as we will see below, the system and its spendthrift habits stem from a "Profits Pact" made between the wealthiest minority of doctors and the insurance companies back in the 1950s. Surgeons and other highly paid specialists softened their opposition to prepaid health plans, which in turn allowed them to charge virtually any price they wanted. We are still living with that historical legacy.

Medical schools exacerbate the situation thoroughly. Students who may be inclined to learn and practice a more humane kind of medicine, who see primary care as a career option, or who—heaven forbid—take seriously the notion of a career in preventive medicine, are routinely belittled by their teachers and fellow students. They are surrounded and taught by science nerds who see all of medicine, indeed the whole of human affairs, as a push-pull, click-click science fair apparatus, a sort of mechanical toy, requiring no more emotion or wisdom than an unusually clever 12-year-old can muster. They are not taught to listen or to teach, to counsel or to comfort. And in all fairness, nobody is willing to pay them to do those things. So what conceivable incentive would they have to learn or to do them?

One of my more enlightening experiences in medical school was with Dr. Edward Cassem, who had been a Jesuit priest before he became a physician and psychiatrist. In a mahogany-paneled sitting room in one of the school's oldest buildings, he taught a group of us "The Four Laws of Medicine":

> If it's working, keep doing it.
> If it's not working, stop doing it.
> If you don't know what to do, don't do anything.
> And never call a surgeon.

The last law was tongue-in-cheek, and I later learned to amend it to the more practical if no less cynical "Never call a surgeon unless you want an operation." But it turns out that in practice the third law is the most important and the most difficult to observe. And today we increasingly realize that its sphere must grow in this country at the expense of the first law, which for too long has dominated clinical practice and third-party payment.

But, you ask, how could it be wrong to keep doing what is working? Answer: if you're merely *imagining* that it's working.

But surely, in medicine, imagination ...

Wrong again. Thanks to the efforts of seasoned medical scientists like John Wennberg of Dartmouth Medical School and younger ones like David Eddy of Duke University, as well as to major studies by the Rand Corporation and others, we now know that only 10 to 20 percent of routinely used medical and surgical procedures in the United States have been proven to work by rigorous studies in randomized controlled trials, the acknowledged gold standard of all medical research and the standard against which all treatments must finally be measured. The result is countless routines of practice adrift from any moorings, and a vast number that are demonstrably unjustified. I remember a young premedical student who, rejecting a primary care career, said, "I want to get out there and *do*." We all tend to identify with surgeons as doers. But what if they turn out to be the ultimate dreamers and bumblers? And what if these dreamy doers, who often have our lives in their hands, frequently do not know what it is they are doing?

The specifics are pretty scary.

John Wennberg did the classic first studies of the tonsillectomy fad of the fifties and sixties. That's right, fad; even to call it a fashion would dignify it too much. Millions of the children who had them (I was one) did not need them. Wennberg, then at the Harvard School of Public Health, studied the rates of tonsil removal in thirteen Vermont areas starting in 1969. In that year, the rate for the U.S. as a whole resembled the Vermont rate. Yet there was a thirteenfold difference between the highest- and lowest-rate districts in the state, an irrational and purposeless variation. These facts were reported back to Vermont doctors through the state medical society, and Vermont began a decline in tonsillectomies that far exceeded the national decline—basically, the fad was ending—that began around the same time. By 1973, the Vermont rate was far lower than the national rate. One district had an *89 percent decline* in five years. Careful analysis led Wennberg and his colleagues to credit the district's sharp drop mainly to feedback—just letting the doctors know how they compared to other doctors. Today tonsillectomies stand at a fraction of what they once were, and kids are better, not worse, off as a result.

I know it's hard to get excited about tonsil removal, and anyway the fad is mostly over (actually, it is estimated that 25 to 30 percent of tonsillectomies today still are unnecessary). But that was only the first example.

A brain bypass operation, introduced in the 1970s, was widely adopted by neurosurgeons for patients with clogged arteries in the neck. It was done thousands of times a year in the 1980s before Dr. Henry Barnett, a neurologist in Canada, decided to study it properly. His international team showed that it did no good, and U.S. third-party payers accordingly stopped paying for it. Barnett's $8 million study thus halted a waste of $250 million a year in the U.S. alone, but not before many thousands of unsuspecting people were subjected to this operation for no scientifically justifiable purpose. This was not the 1930s or the 1950s, but the 1980s.

And what about needless operations today?

Unwarranted hysterectomies have been shown in studies beginning in the 1950s to number, at a minimum, in the scores of thousands yearly. Today half a million a year (warranted and unwarranted)—a hundred thousand fewer than were done fifteen years ago—are done at a cost of $2 billion. Yet a study published in the *Journal of the American Medical Association* in May 1993 showed that in managed care plans— the plans where incentives run against unneeded surgery and where the number of surgeries is supposed to be easier to control—16 percent of hysterectomies still were unjustified. There was little meaningful variation among the seven plans studied, all of which are popular, respected, and financially sound. Kaiser Permanente in both Denver and Pasadena, the Group Health Cooperative of Puget Sound, and the Health Care Plan of Buffalo, New York, were among them.

Contrast this with the experience in the Saskatchewan province of Canada, where surveillance of seven hospitals reduced the number of unjustified hysterectomies by two-thirds, from 24 percent down to 8 percent, between 1970 and 1974. Unnecessary hysterectomies are now approaching the level of honest mistakes in Canada, while in the U.S. we still struggle to rein in knife-happy surgeons even in managed care plans, which supposedly, under the Clinton proposal, are going to be the salvation of our system.

Don't start feeling comfortable just because you're a man. A runaway prostate surgery fad has had older men in its grip for years. The number of radical prostate removals increased sevenfold between 1984 and 1990. But another May 1993 study, published in the *Journal of the American Medical Association,* showed that patients who did not have surgery but were simply followed by their doctors with a wait-and-see attitude fared just as well in terms of survival as those who went under the knife. And that doesn't count complications. Those men who had surgery were often subject to incontinence, bowel obstruction, and impotence. Ouch. And the difference wasn't just with surgery. The wait-and-see attitude was also superior to aggressive radiation treatment in comparable ways and for similar reasons.

How about pacemaker implantation? According to a 1988 article in the *New England Journal of Medicine,* at about thirty Philadelphia-area hospitals, 382 new pacemakers were surgically sewn into heart patients at Medicare expense in 1983. One out of five clearly should not have been implanted. Almost another two in five were questionable. At least three-fourths of the hospitals were seriously at fault. If, as is likely, the Philadelphia area reflects national practice, then we are doing at least 25,000 unwarranted pacemaker implantations yearly.

Or take a look at carotid endarterectomy, a reaming out of the same clogged arteries in the neck that a useless operation once tried to bypass. Both operations claim to prevent stroke. There were 15,000 of these carotid ream jobs done in the U.S. in 1971, 107,000 in 1985. Randomized controlled trials of its value have been equivocal, but surgeons have convinced insurers that it works, so the high rate of the surgery continues to be paid for. But a study published in 1988 found large-scale unjustified use, even according to the surgeons' own criteria. A random sample of 1,302 Medicare patients was drawn from those who received the procedure in three large geographic areas. Thirty-two percent had the operation for clearly inappropriate reasons, and the same percentage again for equivocal reasons. Only 35 percent had it for reasons that clearly met the criteria *set by surgeons themselves.* Even these operations, based on the study data, did not confer benefits that outweighed the risks.

The story is told of a surgeon who, near the end of a successful career, was asked a philosophical question: Would you continue to practice if you won the Florida lottery? The jackpot at the time was $40 million. A thoughtful pause ensued. "Well," the good doctor said, "I would still continue to operate, but I would only do indicated procedures." That means operations that are justified.

The joke is on the doctor, of course, but in the event he did not win the lottery. The major insurance companies did. And the jackpot was not 40 million but hundreds of billions. Hillary Rodham Clinton drew the winning ticket, put a ribbon on it, and sent it to the directors of Cigna, Metropolitan Life, and a handful of other companies. The lottery ticket doesn't just hand them billions of dollars. It also hands them immense new power. These people will use it to take away our choice of doctor, but if their past behavior is any guide, they will not reduce unnecessary surgery.

Abuse of surgery seems particularly egregious, but unwarranted procedures and tests are done in all specialties.

Look at coronary angiograms, an invasive procedure to X-ray the arteries of the heart, and one of the most frequently performed medical procedures in the United States. A study of Medicare patients in three geographic regions recently showed that only about three-fourths of those done were clearly appropriate, and 17 percent were clearly inappropriate. Since this procedure has a small but significant death rate—perhaps 1 in 200 cases—the performance of tens of thousands of needless angiograms must lead to hundreds of needless deaths. It certainly leads to many millions of dollars of needless costs.

There is a simple and fundamental point here that must not be missed. The American health care crisis is not just an undertreatment problem. It is also an overtreatment problem. If you are uninsured, you are missing needed treatments, and you have an increased risk of death and disability because of it. But if you are insured—regardless of whether by an HMO, a PPO, Medicare, or Medicaid—or if you are able to pay out-of-pocket, you are getting unneeded treatments, and you run an increased risk of death or disability because of those treatments. We have too many surgeons doing too many operations, too many other specialists doing too many other procedures, countless patients wronged by them year in and year out, soaring needless costs, and a desperate, worsening dearth of the most needed doctors: the general internists, pediatricians, and family practitioners who serve on the front lines, the real heroes in modern American medicine.

Few cases demonstrate better how overdependence on specialized technology makes today's doctors stupid than that of Franklin Yee, a 58-year-old man with a severe pain in his belly. Yee, who is a surgeon, became nauseous and feverish while playing golf. Because the pain was in his upper abdomen, an electrocardiogram was done. It was normal, but his doctors decided to pursue some slightly questionable squiggles. In the cardiac intensive care unit, Dr. Yee thought back on the thousand or so appendectomies he had done over the years, and he decided he probably had a slightly atypical form of appendicitis. His son, a surgeon-in-training, examined him and agreed with his diagnosis, but they couldn't convince anyone, because all they had to rely on was their clinical experience and judgment.

Hours turned into days while thousands of dollars' worth of tests were ordered. Specialized kidney X-rays, barium studies, CT scans of the abdomen all were done with varying results, but the CT suggested a massive infarction of the intestine, something resembling an intestinal heart attack. Dr. Yee, being rolled into the operating room, ostensibly to have much of his bowel removed, stuck to his original diagnosis. No one believed him, until they opened his belly and found that the inflamed appendix, which he had correctly identified in the first place, had ruptured, seriously endangering not his bowel but his life. His thirty years of clinical knowledge could not penetrate the obsessive self-assurance of his doctors as they pursued their "scientific"—really scientistic—will-o'-the-wisps. The cost of Dr. Yee's treatment was $30,000, at least triple what it should have been.

If Dr. Yee, with all his knowledge and connections, could not save himself from this nerdy, overenthusiastic bumbling, what chance does the average person have of avoiding the substitution of the complex, costly, and dangerous approaches to illness for the simple, cheap, and safe ones? These problems affect every single American. In his speech to the Governors' Association in August 1993, President Clinton gave his former colleagues an updated version of the old Reagan-Bush bromide: Americans have the best health care in the world, and we shouldn't tamper with it. I call this the Ostrich Strategy.

The Clinton version is that Americans *who have access* have the best care in the world. But this is scarcely more true than the Republican version of the platitude. It reflects a dangerous lack of understanding of what is going on at the level of real illness and real medicine. The fact is, Americans who have insurance are getting hundreds of thousands of needless operations and millions of needless tests and medications every year. These unjustified treatments threaten patients' health, their lives, and their bank accounts. They affect us all.

But logic, not just compassion, demands that we look at the group we have completely left out—the poor, whether working or not, whether uninsured or "covered" by Medicaid. Everyone seems to understand that we no longer even pretend to care for the poor. In the late eighties George Bush promised us a kinder, gentler nation, but the most disadvantaged among us live in an ever rougher, more neglectful one. Take Harlem, for instance.

A 1990 article in the *New England Journal of Medicine*, probably the most respected medical periodical, proved what physicians have long suspected: excess mortality in Harlem routinely surpasses that caused by well-publicized natural disasters in other communities. In fact, as the authors—Colin McCord and Harold Freeman, both doctors at Harlem Hospital—state plainly in their summary, "black men in Harlem were less likely to reach the age of sixty-five than men in Bangladesh."

Bangladesh, for those of us who grew up before the widely publicized African famines, has always symbolized the quintessence of the tragedy of underdevelopment—"third-worldness" at its worst. It used to be claimed, in the sixties and seventies, that the underdeveloped world was only a subway ride away. Mere rhetoric, argued the wiser heads of the eighties. But as those wiser heads were cutting taxes and raising military spending, quashing a national health plan and concocting a multibillion-dollar war-in-space adventure, the people of Harlem were languishing in a state that, in terms of health, was and is unmatched by some of the most backward, most deprived, most impoverished nations in the world.

Yet to those who know, this finding was nothing new. Physician-administrators and practitioners at the Centers for Disease Control, state health departments, and big city hospitals all over America reacted to the report without surprise. All of them knew that equally bad conditions obtain in inner-city neighborhoods in every major American city. All of these health care professionals have that slightly tired look of men and women who have pounded on the table too many times; who have made, perhaps, too many personal sacrifices in an era when their peers made cupidity a virtue; and who yet have to pace themselves, protecting their emotions, since they have no intention of abandoning their watches while the war against illness-in-poverty still rages. No, no one who knows is surprised. But the unusually blunt language in the world's most widely respected medical journal turned a long-standing domestic embarrassment into an international disgrace.

Well, you might say, maybe these Harlem doctors fiddled with the statistics. You would be wrong. The numbers are simple, and are worse than they appear at first glance. Because of the need to compare Harlem with the latest national census data, the study focused on 1980 and the year preceding and following it. In the three years under study—and remember, this was 1979–81, before the age of AIDS—2,421 people in Harlem died needlessly. That is more than 800 people a year beyond the number that would have died if Harlem shared the health of the nation. It is, for instance, more than the annual death count in the Palestinian intifada. But now that the intifada is only a bad memory, the excess deaths in Harlem will keep right on occurring. Eight hundred a year. The number of deaths in the San Francisco earthquake of 1989 was 67; in hurricanes Hugo and Andrew, 62 and 85 respectively; and in the great Midwestern floods of the summer of 1993, an estimated 50.

Mortality declined for U.S. whites from 1960 to 1980, and it declined even more steeply for U.S. nonwhites. But in Harlem, mortality stayed the same or rose slightly during the same period. For

Harlem males, the likelihood of reaching any age older than forty is lower than that for males in the state of Matlab, Bangladesh.

In the third world, low life expectancy is caused mainly by very high infant mortality, a statistic that has improved even in Harlem. So if you look at life expectancy *after* childhood, it is better in Bangladesh than in Harlem, for women just as for men. Male or female, if you are an adult, your chances of dying in any given future year until age sixty-five are higher in Harlem than in Matlab.

Well, you say, this is not really about health. It's about things like homicide and drug abuse, things that people bring on themselves. You would be wrong there too. True enough, homicide rates were much higher in Harlem than the national average, but they account for only 15 percent of the excess deaths; cancer caused almost as high a proportion. Drug dependency, it is true, caused far more deaths in Harlem than in the nation, yet this highly visible problem contributed only 7 percent of the excess deaths. All in all, the leading cause of excess death in Harlem was plain, dull cardiovascular disease—also the leading killer in the nation as a whole. The peak ages of vulnerability, when death rates were about six times higher across the board, also did not support a drugs-and-violence theory. For women, the worst ages for excess death from all causes were twenty-five to thirty-four; for men, thirty-five to forty-four. Violence and drugs kill younger.

Don't picture drug dealers blowing each other away. Picture a 33-year-old mother of three, disgusted with a crowded and dangerous emergency room and needing to get back home to her children. Some weeks later, her uncontrolled high blood pressure leads to a devastating stroke. Or, picture a man of forty-five—all right, make him a smoker—whose crushing chest pain drops him on his way to find a job. Picture a 60-year-old diabetic going blind from lack of treatment, who stumbles out in front of a fast-moving bus.

And don't make the mistake of thinking Harlem is special. A 1991 study in East Baltimore showed twice the rate of blindness in blacks as in whites, and that was only for people under the age of sixty-five. As Dr. Johanna Seddon concluded, "Among the poor, a lack of access to care and a lack of trust in medical care providers often result in a delay ... that can cause conditions to reach a point where they are more difficult to treat and cure."

If you are poor, of course, this process may cost you your sight. But if you are not poor, it *will* cost you money. The reasons are not difficult to follow.

There is plenty of evidence that the differences in health, illness, care, and mortality described above are more a function of poverty and neglect than of race itself. For the purposes of the health economy, poverty must be defined as either uninsured or insured by Medicaid. A 1992 study in the *Journal of the American Medical Association* showed that in Massachusetts and Maryland, both the uninsured and Medicaid patients have much higher rates of hospitalization than other groups for conditions that could have been avoided with timely care outside the hospital, the kind of care such patients either cannot afford or have no access to. Prominent among these conditions are asthma, congestive heart failure, diabetes, and gangrene.

Privately insured patients with these conditions have access to physicians who, at much smaller expense, take regular care of the patients and keep them out of the hospital. Uninsured and Medicaid patients have no such monitoring, and so end up in the hospital much more frequently. And these differences persist after correcting for race, poverty, and alcoholism; of two white males with the same income and the same drinking habits, the one who is uninsured will fare much worse. So the simple result is that patients who could have been kept out of the hospital at low expense end up inside the hospital at high expense. But only some hospitals will take them.

Who would turn away a person at the hospital door who cannot breathe, or who is in a diabetic coma, or in severe pain, for lack of means? You'd be surprised. Overall, 250,000 seriously ill patients a year are turned away from or out of American hospitals and told to go elsewhere, an estimated 87 percent of them for lack of means. This evil practice of "patient dumping" continues even where laws have severely restricted it. Ask Jerrill Palmer, who at age two lost his mother when a Georgia hospital turned her away in July 1990. She was nine months pregnant, nauseous, and suffering from excruciating abdominal pain. They didn't even examine her. She went out, ruptured her uterus, and died along with her baby.

The burden on families created by such maltreatment of women is, of course, enormous. A study published in the *New England Journal of Medicine* in July 1993 looked at 4,675 women in New Jersey who had invasive breast cancer before the age of sixty-five. Those who were uninsured or insured by Medicaid were at least 40 percent more likely to die than patients with private insurance. The differences were greatest in women who initially had disease that had not spread to distant parts of the body. These are the women who should have had the best chance of survival. But the uninsured and Medicaid patients just didn't get good follow-up care, a crucial part of breast cancer treatment. On the way to their unnecessary deaths, these women used up enormous resources for fruitless treatments that no longer had a chance of saving them. Remember, too, that they were women in the prime of life, many of whom left children behind to create further economic and social burdens.

The medical profession has long claimed that once they come to the hospital, poor patients are cared for every bit as well as rich ones. It just isn't so. A 1992 study in New York State showed that the uninsured are more than twice as likely as the privately insured to be victimized by substandard care leading to medical injury.

A few examples:

A man comes to the hospital after an auto accident. He has symptoms suggesting spinal damage in his neck. X-rays are done, but no one looks at them. He is discharged, gets much worse, goes to another hospital later that day, and is found to have a serious dislocation of a vertebra, a life- and limb-threatening condition.

A young woman comes to an emergency room with belly pain, but without fever or vaginal discharge. She is treated for pelvic infection and sent home. A pregnancy test is ordered and comes back positive, but nobody checks it. Three days later she comes back with severe belly pain and needs emergency surgery for an ectopic pregnancy, a life- and fertility-threatening condition.

A woman with anemia is seen occasionally at a clinic over a two-year period, but never has her anemia evaluated. She eventually comes in with a ruptured intestine and is found to have metastatic colon cancer, now a deadly condition.

The list goes on. These things can happen to the insured also, but the point is they are more than twice as likely to happen to the uninsured. I am not asking you to shed any tears for the uninsured, even though the human cost of their substandard treatment is colossal. I am asking you to think like a practical man or woman. Are you prepared to turn these people away when they come back with their dreadful diseases, worsened by sloppy care or no care at all? If your answer is no, then you are being victimized by an enormous waste of your money, due to the failure to provide decent, timely care in advance of the crisis—care that would cost less and do far more.

If early intervention is inadequate, preventive measures are still more neglected. At present, the principle that guides us seems to be, "a dollar's worth of cure is better than a penny's worth of prevention." So if you want an inoculation, a prenatal exam, a cholesterol or blood pressure check, a rectal exam, or a mammogram, you're usually on your own, even though these measures, when properly done, save money and eliminate untold suffering. Our philosophy in America seems to be that individuals must take these responsibilities on themselves. But what most Americans miss is the fact that we don't take them on ourselves, and instead we show up at the hospital door with all the diseases these measures could have prevented. And at that point the bill for fix-it treatments, very often futile, is truly something to behold.

THE

CAUSE

SINCE ANCIENT TIMES, we have had a love-hate relationship with our doctors; they have alternately been seen as the noblest and the most scurrilous of professionals. We are all ambivalent about doctors because of their great power over us. The ancient teachers of medicine understood this, and that is why the Hippocratic Oath, the Physician's Prayer of Maimonides, the ancient Hindu commandments to medical graduates, and other medical documents and rituals formally swear physicians to the highest possible ethical standard. What is at stake is public trust, without which a doctor is merely a quack.

Yet, ironically, it was not until more than two millennia after the young Greek and Hindu physicians first swore to keep their patients' welfare at the top of their list of priorities that physicians could be relied upon to consistently do more good than harm. At the dawn of the twentieth century, great advances in science had made medicine more than a craft for the first time in history. Pasteur had blazed new paths to the conquest of ancient plagues. Rudolf Virchow had founded the science of pathology, showing how each disease wreaks its special havoc in the body. Paul Ehrlich had discovered the first cure for an infectious scourge, syphilis, and coined the phrase "silver bullet" to capture the cure's almost magical effect. William Osler, successively a leader of medicine in Canada, the United States, and Britain, had written the first great textbook of medicine and established the method of thinking about disease and teaching at the bedside that is universal today.

These advances in medical science led to the first great *social* transformation of medicine. Until the early twentieth century, physicians could be trained either in medical schools or as apprentices. There were no effective laws regulating quackery. If you could convince people that you were a medical miracle worker and that snake oil was just the thing, more power to you. But by early this century groups of well-trained doctors with increasingly professional identities had the confidence to pressure state legislatures to license and regulate medical practices. This effort was to their credit, but also to their advantage. They were establishing an exclusive set of prerogatives.

During the next half-century the American people gave doctors virtually blind trust and doctors used it well. They had maximum independence and with it did a great deal of good. They developed lifesaving operations, rigorously improved sterile conditions in hospitals, dramatically reduced infant and maternal mortality, introduced antibiotics and vaccines that brought a halt to terrifying diseases, and stood steadfastly between the human mind and the age-old curse of pain. This was American medicine's Golden Age. It lasted until about 1960.

In the wake of the Second World War came many political and social changes, one of which was the first proposed major change in the organization of medicine since it was fully professionalized at the turn of the century. The concept of guaranteed medical care for every citizen was sweeping the civilized world.

The United States was at first no exception to this trend. In 1937, health reform was already front page news as the *New York Times* of Sunday, November 7, reported, "National Policy on Health Asked by 430 Doctors." These doctors, including leading practitioners, teachers, and medical school deans, held to four principles:

- that the health of the people is a direct concern of the government

- that national public health policy, directed toward all groups of the population, should be formulated

- that the problem of economic need and the problem of providing adequate medical care are not identical and may require different approaches for their solution

- that four agencies are concerned in the provision of adequate medical care: voluntary agencies, and local, state, and federal governments

The doctors also made specific proposals favoring prevention programs and public funding of care for the indigent, as well as for medical research, education, and public health. They specifically doubted the ability of health insurance alone to solve the major existing problems.

Today these ideas are widely accepted. Their time has come. But at the time the group of 430 doctors met with immediate and vigorous opposition from the American Medical Association (AMA), and especially from the editor of its journal, Dr. Morris Fishbein, whose name must go down in history as synonymous with doctors' obstructionist role in preventing health reform. With the support of a self-serving board he consistently editorialized against all proposals for reform. He had a daily newspaper column as well as a journal, and he rejected even such modest ideas as group practice and voluntary prepayment plans. In flourishes of sophomoric rhetoric he called government involvement in medicine totalitarian, sorely misrepresented its impact in other countries, and invoked Abraham Lincoln to support his claim that "no people can exist with a medical profession enslaved to make a politician's holiday." Dr. John Peters, a professor of medicine at Yale, rebutted Fishbein point-by-point in a much more balanced address delivered to the American College of Physicians the following year.

But the AMA blitz had done its damage. The subject was not raised again in a formal way until after the war, when Harry Truman, carrying out a clear intention of Franklin Roosevelt's, made national health reform a goal of his presidency. He announced his plan on

November 19, 1945, and Fishbein's AMA immediately launched an all-out war of words and dollars against it. Truman's was an excellent plan for decentralized insurance and free choice of doctors, and it would have saved America decades of unnecessary pain, including the current mess that passes for a debate on health reform. But the AMA killed it at birth, even hiring a team of media consultants to orchestrate a national campaign against Truman's dream.

Harry Truman's original proposal, far from being a herald of totalitarianism and slavery, was, in fact, part of a successful international movement to bring decency, fairness, and rationality to the chaos of health care delivery. In 1946 Britain began its National Health Service. In 1947 Sweden adopted compulsory universal health insurance, although unlike Britain it did not nationalize its hospitals or put its doctors on salary. France began in 1945 to expand health insurance, covering 99 percent of its population by 1967. Norway adopted universal coverage in 1956; Denmark expanded its coverage gradually, reaching universal compulsory insurance in 1971. West Germany, Austria, Italy, the Netherlands, and Belgium enacted laws that steadily expanded coverage, eventually making it universal.

In Canada, the evolution of universal care began in 1947 with the introduction of public hospital insurance in Saskatchewan. British Columbia, Alberta, and Newfoundland followed with modified versions of hospital coverage in 1949. The Canadian Parliament enacted a federal assistance program to share the cost of the provincial plans in 1957. Care outside the hospital was again first covered in Saskatchewan, in 1962. With federal assistance beginning in 1968, all of the provinces were able to enact universal public coverage of hospital and out-of-hospital services by 1972. Then, as now, the single payer was at the provincial level, with a very small coordinating office in Ottawa. Unlike in Britain, doctors in Canada have remained independent professionals and even entrepreneurs, except where they have chosen to affiliate in large group practices—much less prominent with Canadian doctors than among their colleagues to the south.

Meanwhile, back in the U.S.A., a pervasive culture of rugged individualism and institutionalized greed ("market values") was, with the help of the conservative doctors who dominated the AMA, taking us in a very different direction. True, there were incremental changes even here—government funding of research and eventually Medicare and Medicaid. But the overall trend, compared with the rest of the world, was all engines full speed in reverse.

The main reason for this backwardness, other than rigid opposition to change from organized medicine, was the lure of big profits for commercial insurance companies. Early in the century they had successfully blocked government-sponsored coverage, and by mid-century these efforts had started to pay off. Blue Cross, and then Blue Shield, had emerged before World War II as nonprofit protection for some individuals against unexpected hospital and medical expenses. Henry Kaiser had started his Permanente plans for workers in his war-related industries, which took a more direct approach to providing medical services. But it was not until after the war that corporate insurance interests saw they could reap big profits from the approach that the nonprofit Blues had pioneered.

At first, organized medicine—the AMA, still headed by Fishbein—vigorously opposed all forms of group practice and all forms of insurance. The claim was that any move away from solo practice and fee-for-service private payment would lead to bad medicine, period. But they changed their tune drastically during the fifties, and began to sing in harmony with the big new corporate interests in health insurance.

These companies were growing rapidly. They institutionalized the link between jobs and coverage by selling plans to large employers, at first with the backing of big unions. They soon realized that their profits would be greater if they enrolled more people who were less likely to be or to get sick, and so they invented "experience rating" to bias prices and enrollment in favor of the youngest, healthiest groups. This practice has come down to us as "cherry picking," the drive by profit-hungry insurers to build up panels of members who are and will stay well.

The AMA played a role in all this that would be fascinating if it were not so sleazy. After decades of unbending opposition to insurance, the AMA began to realize that these corporate interests were marketing health care in a way the AMA never could, bringing an enormous infusion of new capital into the health economy. During the fifties, what I call a tacit "Profits Pact" emerged between the AMA and these new corporate interests. In effect, the AMA said to the corporate insurers: We will relax our opposition to your involvement in medicine as long as you guarantee us a secure and ever-expanding income base, and keep your hands off our professional prerogatives. The corporate interests said: Fine, just don't squawk when we cream our profits off the top.

Both sides of this deal proved extremely lucrative, but it had two major flaws. First, it didn't just leave out a third or so of America's citizens, it actually made things worse for them. As in the past, their only option was to pay out-of-pocket. But the Profits Pact was inflating costs at an unprecedented speed. As long as the insurance companies could raise premiums faster than doctors raised prices, they could count on increased profits. Uninsured patients were emptying their pockets before they could get the care they needed. The older they were, the poorer they were, the sicker they were, and the more vulnerable they were, the less likely they were to get either insurance against disaster or care when disaster finally struck.

Second, doctors would eventually discover the risks and costs of bedding down with the corporate devil: the people who paid the piper—that is, the insurance companies that paid the medical bills—could and would call the tune. It took a decade or two for corporate insurers to get the upper hand, but this they did. And then physicians found that they sat on an organizational totem pole below career managers and business school wonks who not only had never been to medical school, but had never had a moment's responsibility for the care of a sick human being. These people's responsibilities, such as they were, were quite different: payroll, stockholders, and, of course, profits. By 1980 physicians had begun to feel like the Native Americans of Manhattan who sold rights to use the island for a boxful of trinkets and only later realized that they had sold and forfeited their birthright.

Back in the early sixties doctors were still in control, but people were growing increasingly disgusted with the plight of those who were left out. The poor themselves may not have been powerful, but they had some influential populist allies. And the elderly were increasingly numerous, they voted more than younger people, and they too were infected by the zeitgeist of standing up and demanding their rights. The combined result was Medicare for the elderly and Medicaid for the poorest of the poor. These programs, also opposed with tremendous force by the AMA, were the centerpieces of Lyndon Johnson's Great Society program. For the elderly, Medicare would, in time, provide a fairly good set of benefits, protected and extended by the recipients' enormous voting power. For the poor, Medicaid would provide a floor below which they would not be allowed to fall. A low floor, but a floor. The poor would not be left to die in the street nor cast onto the charity rolls of increasingly cash-hungry doctors. In a touching irony, Johnson signed the Medicare bill into law in the presence of Harry Truman, who must have relished greatly his belated partial victory over his old enemies in the AMA.

But doing reform in a piecemeal way had problems of its own. The AMA did not actually boycott Medicare, but doctors resisted it, steered clear of it when they could, and occasionally even abused or defrauded it. During the seventies a two-tiered system of health care emerged, with not only the poor but also the increasingly vast population of elderly in the lower tier. The Profits Pact between commercial insurers and the wealthier class of doctors continued, and consumers who could afford it got "the best" care. (The reason this phrase needs to be in quotes is that, as we know, these well-heeled patients increasingly got too much treatment, and too much treatment is by no means the best.) Meanwhile, Medicare inevitably brought up the rear in terms of both physician payment (the amount and the promptness) and prestige. Doctors hated the growing hassles they suffered at the hands of all the bean counters, paper pushers, and phone jockeys, but they hated the government version most of all.

The great beneficiaries of the changes of the seventies were for-profit corporations making a fast buck on sick people. Drug industry sales and profits were ahead of all other industries, and drug price inflation began (and continues) to be not only far ahead of the Consumer Price Index but even ahead of medical cost inflation generally. HMOs began the expansion that would take off in the eighties, and efforts by the Nixon administration, ever pro-corporation, strongly fostered this development.

During this decade, too, as Paul Starr has shown, profit-making hospital chains first came into their own. Hospital Corporation of America (HCA) rose from ownership of 23 hospitals in 1970 (when it was the largest chain) to over 300 in 1981. Humana, Inc., which proudly compared its ambitions for its products to those of McDonald's hamburgers, was a $4.8 million nursing home company in Louisville in 1968. In 1980 its 92 hospitals generated $1.4 billion and its stock had gone from $8 to $336. The stockholders were no doubt dancing for joy, but the American people paid the band.

Corporate insurance was inclined to be favorable to this devel-opment. As a 1980 article in *Fortune*, "Humana's Hard-Sell Hospi-tals," put it, "Privately insured patients can be charged what the market will bear." As for uninsured or inadequately insured patients, except in emergency they were out of luck. As profit-making hospital enterprises diversified and became conglomerates, they were less and less identified with the needs of patients or the professionalism of doctors. At the end of the 1970s, Dr. Arnold Relman, then editor-in-chief of the *New England Journal of Medicine*, introduced the term "medical–industrial complex" to describe the process of corporatization and the rise of market values. He presciently warned that in time the process would seriously damage both physicians' professional interest and their public trust.

Then came the eighties, when the country went into denial and the worship of mammon became respectable for the first time in over half a century. In 1970 only 40 percent of college freshmen had listed "Be very well off financially" as a major life goal, while almost 80 percent cited "Develop a meaningful philosophy of life." By the late eighties these percentages were precisely reversed. The money-making heroes of the decade—Charles Keating, Ivan Boesky, Michael Milken, Donald Trump, Leona Helmsley, Neil Bush (the president's son), and many lesser lights—were by the end of it either in jail or in a state of public and financial humiliation and powerlessness. Unfortunately they were only the tip of the iceberg of sanctimonious greed that America's economy and values soon foundered on. Neither commercial insurers nor doctors, corporate hospital-owners nor malpractice litigators, drug company managers nor HMO stockholders—none were immune to the "greed is good" cultural process that threatened to freeze out compassion and fairness. The main event of the eighties was a free-style dash for cash, and no one wanted to be left behind. Health sector inflation far outstripped that of the economy, drug price inflation outstripped even that, and most of the windfall went into the pockets of a few tens of thousands of wealthy people.

This sickness-as-business attitude continues to dominate the corporate sector of the health economy. Morley Safer of "60 Minutes" told a chilling story on the *New York Times* Op-Ed page recently. An investment banker, the son of an old friend, called to drum up business. Safer told him he was exceptionally cautious and that he would only consider "something brass-bottomed safe and profitable." A few days later a letter came recommending stock in a medical business. "The company's potential customer base is small but lucrative: 20,000 hemophiliacs and others afflicted by rare but lifelong diseases." Similar companies had frequent patient turnover, the letter argued, but the recommended one "treats individuals for which no cures exist. As a result, once patients sign on with the company, a recurring revenue stream is created that can last for decades. A hemophiliac, for example, must pay about $50,000 a year for treatment." Furthermore, wrote the counselor, "because of the relatively captive nature of the company's customer base, the prediction to buy at the current price is on line."

Safer's own comment is trenchant: "America's approach to health care defies not only logic and compassion, it defies gravity. Here we have the perfect example of the trickle-up theory.... Not only is greed good, but ... its balance sheet is healthy." This is the sickness business at its most shameless, but it is not absurd because it is happening—today.

Still, to some extent the monster of greed began to run out of energy in the nineties, and as it moved more slowly across the landscape, Americans could appreciate how ugly it really was. Doctors had dropped so far in prestige that no one cared what they thought any more—a far cry from the era when they could call all the shots. Insurance companies were gobbling up HMOs, with Prudential, Aetna, Cigna, and Metropolitan Life achieving complete vertical integration (read "vertical monopoly") on health care. As one Wall Street analyst put it, "I envision the insurance companies transforming themselves into HMOs or getting out of the business." Cigna, to take one example, is immersed in what the *New York Times* called "a bet-the-company drive to become a dominant force in the new world of 'managed care' health plans," and "rushing to organize networks that they hope will generate big money for decades to come."

Has Cigna helped shape the Clinton plan to protect those future profits? You bet your health it has. How? The Clintons aim to create vast new markets for the very HMOs that Cigna and other insurers are buying. All of us now independent of HMOs, comfortable with our present doctors, will be forced to make deals with the likes of the new, enlarged Cigna, deals that will allow us to switch to any doctor of their choice. We'll pay them the premium, they'll choose the doctor, and the doctor, who will work for them, will of course follow their orders. The new Cigna—or Prudential, or Aetna, or Metropolitan Life—will do it all. Today, with the Clinton plan on the horizon, insurance-company ownership of HMOs, hospitals, and other health facilities is growing by leaps and bounds, and commercial insurance, once a weak little backwater industry, is poised to take over a seventh of the American economy, subordinate doctors completely to nonmedical managers, and leave the ill, whether rich or poor, at the mercy of their corporate profit motive.

So the forties were the Decade of AMA Dominance, when organized medicine said no to every reform and got away with it, leaving the United States in the dust as the civilized world surged forward in health care.

The fifties were the Decade of the Profits Pact, when health-insurance-for-profit corporations and the top politicians of the medical profession shook hands across a big pot of gold.

The sixties were the Decade of Piecemeal Reform, when the country became repulsed at the unfairness of the system and the government began to shield both the elderly and the poorest of the poor from the powerful moneyed interests that were hurting their health.

The seventies were the Decade of Corporate Expansion, when physicians were going into retreat and giving up their independence to an ever-swelling army of paper pushers, bean counters, and phone jockeys, and when it began to dawn on Americans that we could not sustain forever a system in which costs were out of control.

And the eighties were the Decade of Unbridled Greed. Corporate giants swallowed hundreds of hospitals and thoroughly proletarianized physicians; malpractice lawyers pitted patients against doctors, with their sights on absurd damage awards; and physicians, increasingly outraged by their new subordinate position and foreseeing even worse to come, resolved, before the chance was gone forever, to take whatever was not nailed down.

This, then, is the sad history that has brought us to our present pass amid the charged hopes and fears of the nineties. How will the future refer to this decade? We have no way of knowing. What we do know is that America's health care system, far from being the envy of the world as it once was, is now the world's unremitting embarrassment. That the poor are without decent care and the middle class are constantly afraid. That doctors have declined drastically in public esteem, and are the objects of constant legal and journalistic assault. That our priorities in health care are topsy-turvy, made that way by the weight of a pigheaded fix-it mentality. And that the people most responsible for every part of this mess, the corporate interests who have lined their pockets with our precious health care dollars, have made their grip on the system all but permanent.

Special interests abound, of course, but some need singling out. The worst are corporate medicine and corporate health insurers. These are the people who have entered medicine for one reason: profits. They make no bones about it, but they claim that this is best for everyone. There is no reason to think this is a true claim, but they can afford to repeat it in full-page ads and television spots—the "big lie" technique that has worked so often in the past. They are the major obstacle to real change—except of course for change that will enhance their market position.

The Clintons' health reform plan is just such a change.

Corporate medicine experienced explosive profits growth in the eighties, a windfall from outrageous inflation and useless growth. Duplication of services may have hurt the commonweal, but it certainly didn't hurt the corporation. Drug profits took off, and what was reinvested went more for promotion—often illegitimate promotion—than for research. For-profit hospital chains experienced enormous growth that made their gains of the 1970s look weak. HMOs quadrupled their enrollment to 40 million people, while PPOs went from almost zero to 18 million. These people do not want any reforms that might tend to threaten their markets.

For-profit health insurance corporations are more powerful than they have ever been. For all the talk about government involvement and government bureaucracy, almost $300 billion of the $643 billion we spent on health care in 1990 was controlled by corporate sources of payment. Government accounted for $213 billion, and out-of-pocket payments $136 billion. In August 1993, President Clinton estimated that commercial insurers would collect $500 billion in premiums for the year. The 1991 salaries of the top executives of ten insurance companies ranged from $648,000 to $2,396,000. Countless lower-ranking executives made lesser but still absurdly large amounts of money. These people have an immense amount to lose if corporate insurers fail to preserve the status quo—money that could be used to enhance the lives of the American people. But these millionaire paper pushers are dominating the current White House reform process, and if the Clinton reforms pass they will have even more money.

Third on the list of special interests are the richest 20 percent of doctors. Only a small minority of doctors commit outright fraud, but a much larger minority are engaged in practices more appropriate for the fashion industry or the used car business than for medicine. They may have become doctors for the best reasons, but somewhere along the way they decided that major wealth was a suitable goal for a person whose job is caring for the sick. Thousands of them make half a million, a million dollars, or more each year. They blacken the name of all other doctors, even of medicine itself, and they are to blame for much of the loss of trust doctors have suffered at the end of the twentieth century. They deem it ethical to invest in facilities to which they then refer patients, a practice equivalent to fee-splitting. They control the American Medical Association and use it to further their interests, which are not the same as the interests of doctors in general. On the contrary, primary care doctors suffer more than anyone at the hands of these high-tech cowboys who, in effect, drain off vast wealth that should be redistributed among primary care physicians, who are very often struggling to make ends meet. We will never attract the number of front-line doctors we desperately need without improving the quality of life this profession offers. If average doctors, especially primary care doctors, ever wake up to the need to sever their ties to these wealthy colleagues whose interests are so different from their own, they will become a powerful force for change.

Fourth in importance among the special interests are the major pharmaceutical corporations, who whine constantly about the cost of research but actually spend far more on dubious promotion. Their profit-taking and price increases in the past decade have been unconscionable, far ahead of other industries. In 1992 they had an estimated $10 billion profit on sales of $76 billion, a profit margin of 13 percent. Top executives in six leading companies in 1991 made salaries ranging from $1,979,000 to $12,788,000. Think about those fellows the next time your heart beats fast in astonishment at the local pharmacy cash register.

I understand their claims about research very well. Only a minority of those research efforts are worthwhile. Most of their research is directed toward producing "me too" drugs that offer no advance over what we have, and then launching misleading promotion campaigns that confuse both doctors and patients. Many of the drugs they introduce are positively dangerous and should not be prescribed. But these people will do everything they have to do to protect their financial interests, and for them that means protecting the status quo.

According to Dr. Sidney Wolfe, head of a respected Washington public interest group that, among other things, evaluates drugs for consumers, 104 of the 287 most frequently prescribed drugs are too dangerous to use. Many more are of questionable value or duplicate, at greater expense, the effects of older tried-and-true drugs. The avidity of drug company salespeople, their high-pressure sales techniques, the aggressiveness of their advertising, and the non-public-spirited nature of their activities exacerbate misprescribing, which is a major factor in health care waste. The thousands of dollars *per physician* spent by pharmaceutical firms every year to convey their biased message makes objective medical decision-making difficult.

A study published in the *Annals of Internal Medicine* in June 1992 showed how misleading drug company claims can be. Scientific experts (more than 100 medical scientists and more than fifty pharmacists) reviewed 109 full-page drug ads from medical journals. More than half the ads were judged to be misleading enough that they should never have been published in reputable journals. More than 90 percent of the ads were judged to violate FDA standards in some way. And many other drug company promotions are strictly beyond legal standards. In 1988 alone sixteen companies sponsored 34,688 symposia, at a total cost of $85.9 million. Such events often include subtly misleading claims that tend to the sponsoring company's advantage. But there is no way for the FDA to monitor all of them. In addition, outright gifts, parties, and junkets for physicians are deliberately used by the companies to soften doctors' judgment.

With all these misleading promotions in the air, it is not surprising that public trust in pharmaceutical science has suffered. Alternative remedies, with all their wasteful cost and risk, may strike the consumer as no worse than an overpromoted prescription drug. A whole network of illegal pharmacies has grown up around AIDS victims, creating a black market in useless and dangerous illegal drugs. And millions of Americans, dismayed by bloated drug company claims, have turned in frustration to completely untested and potentially harmful herbal remedies. Yet pharmaceutical firms show no willingness to reconsider their promotional tactics, their executive salaries, their profit margins, or their pricing policies. They just want to slow down reform.

Fifth in line among special interests are malpractice litigators, the snipers of the system, crouched on the sidelines with high-powered weapons. They are a hidden special interest who have much to lose if significant change occurs. They claim that they keep bad doctors in line and compensate wronged patients—two tasks that they actually do only minimally, and with incredible inefficiency. In fact, they place an enormous financial and human burden on the health care system. They work for contingency fees, counting on the vulnerability of patients, the medical ignorance of juries, and the deep pockets of liability insurers. There are no limits to the awards they can get. Estimates of the total cost of their antics vary, but all are very high. Joseph Califano, a former secretary of Health, Education, and Welfare (now Health and Human Services) and an attorney himself, estimated that in 1991, malpractice insurance premiums alone would cost $10 billion, and that unnecessary tests and procedures by doctors, designed only to derail a future possible malpractice action, would cost $30 billion more.

My observations of doctors in practice suggest that this latter figure is very low. There are several possible reasons for an unnecessary test or procedure. One may be physician gain, another the fact that a third party is paying, and yet another a sort of nervousness on the part of both physician and patient that identifies the best medicine with doing everything conceivable. When an unnecessary procedure is done—and there are hundreds of thousands a year—it is often difficult to say exactly what combination of factors has motivated it. But I know hundreds of practicing doctors, and I know they are scared. A doctor who is sued is already a loser, regardless of the ultimate outcome in the courts. A hospital chaplain I know counsels doctors in this situation, and she describes a consistent pattern of emotional devastation even in doctors who know they have done nothing wrong. The fear of such an event among the masses of physicians is deep and real and justified. Warren E. Burger, former chief justice of the United States, wrote in 1991 of the "litigation explosion": "The consequences of the explosion have become painfully obvious. Suits against hospitals and doctors, which went up 300-fold since the 1970s, increased doctors' medical insurance premiums more than 30-fold for some." What *Forbes* magazine calls "the tort tax"—tort costs as a percentage of gross national product (GNP)—ranges from a low of 0.3 percent in Australia to 0.7 percent in Switzerland. All advanced countries are in this range except the U.S. Here the rate is 2.5 percent, about five times the level of Canada or France.

No wonder protecting themselves, by doing more and more and more, is almost a reflex among today's doctors. And the link between their fear and unnecessary procedures is no longer speculative. A study of acute care hospitals in New York State, published in the *Journal of the American Medical Association* in January 1993, showed that, given the same clinical situation, cesarean section is much more likely where malpractice claims are high. Our national rate of cesarean sections, almost one in four births, is about four times that of Dublin, Ireland, which has lower infant and maternal mortality than we do. Fear of lawsuits, no factor at all in Ireland, is one of the main reasons for our absurd excess of these surgical births.

Don't doctors who make mistakes have to answer for them? Don't the wronged patients deserve compensation? Of course. But look at the way some other countries do this—countries without the American tradition of holier-than-thou litigation. The United States has thirty times as many lawsuits as Japan, per capita. We have two-and-a-half engineers for every lawyer; Japan has twenty. Could this be why they're winning the economic war? In our system, only the lawyers win big. According to a Rand Corporation study, plaintiffs end up with 43 percent of lawsuit winnings; the rest goes for lawyers and court costs.

Sweden has a no-fault system where compensation is far more likely for the victims of medical mishaps than it is here. The awards are smaller but they are substantial, and they are paid to a vastly higher proportion of those wronged. Believe it or not, 70 percent of the claims are supported by the doctors involved in the cases. How can this be? Easy: no-fault. The doctor does not have to be proven negligent for the patient to collect. The Compensation Board pays the patient while a completely different agency, the Medical Responsibility Board, investigates medical wrongdoing. This board has strong consumer representation and only one physician member. Could we do it here? Well, we already do it very well in workers' compensation, automobile insurance, high school sports injuries plans, and children's vaccine injuries. No-fault insurance works. It's just that the trial lawyers don't want you to know that it works.

Malpractice litigators are probably the smallest, numerically, of the greedy and inflationary forces arrayed against change in health care. But they are very influential. Being lawyers, they are vociferous and aggressive in presenting their misleading case. They appeal to the Constitution's seventh amendment, the right to redress of grievances, in much the way the National Rifle Association appeals to the second amendment's right to bear arms. Both groups distort the Bill of Rights and imperil the welfare and safety of the nation. Also, because they are lawyers, malpractice litigators have a disproportionately effective voice in the White House and Congress, both always dense with lawyers. Finally, they appeal egregiously to the tendency of Americans to settle everything with a confrontation.

The most surprising obstacle to reform, however, has been coverage of the issue in the major media, which have offered almost a knee-jerk rejection of the single payer option for several years. I speak not of the conservative press, which can be expected to have brain-stem-level reflexes in such matters. I mean the liberal press, large portions of which knuckled under to the forces behind managed competition when open discussion had barely begun. Reports in these media have consistently misrepresented the structure and function of the Canadian health care system, exaggerated its weaknesses while glossing over its strengths, confused it with the British system of true socialized medicine—an elementary error—and depicted managed competition as the only health reform option worth taking seriously.

The leading offender in these misleading journalistic depictions has been the *New York Times*, probably the most important newspaper in the world. On October 10, 1992, the *Times* stated in its main editorial column, "The debate over health care reform is over. Managed competition has won."

In fact, at that time the debate had barely started. The presidential election still lay ahead and might have confirmed a Republican plan for cosmetic changes only. As for the debate among Democrats and others, few people knew what managed competition was, fewer still understood it (even today it remains the most confusing of major programs), and most Americans were open to learning as much as possible about a *variety* of solutions to the health care crisis. Why then would a distinguished newspaper attempt to quash debate when so much could be gained for the public good by continuing and stimulating it?

The answer may be distressingly simple. As shown in recent research by Jennifer Bauduy, a graduate student at Columbia University, the *New York Times* has been much less fair to the single payer approach than have the *Washington Post* and other leading newspapers. She also shows that the *Times* is intimately bound up with the special interests that stand to gain most from managed competition. Four members of its board of directors—of a total of fourteen, which includes two members of the owners' family—are directors of insurance companies as well. One of these is also CEO of Bristol-Meyers Squibb, "a diversified healthcare company" and pharmaceutical maker. A fifth *Times* director is also on the Bristol-Meyers board. (Judith Sulzberger, a director who belongs to the publisher's family, is a physician.) For a newspaper of this stature to have a board of directors so heavily laden with health industry leaders seems a bit odd. But for that newspaper then to stand out among major liberal media organs for its bias in favor of one particular solution to health reform—the same one that may greatly profit some of those board members—seems simply compromising.

Then, of course, there are the lobbyists, those openly self-interested designers of Washington gridlock. There are thousands of them, they are highly paid, and their job is to take up the time of senators, congressional representatives, and government officials by regularly drubbing them with special interest messages. They pay for this privilege, in ways that the average American cannot afford to. Recently two Democratic senators deeply involved in health reform held a forum for 200 lobbyists, each of whom paid $5,000 for the privilege to attend. It gave the lobbyists a nice chance to get to know some senators, Cabinet members, and White House officials. See, they might want to call those folks up sometime for a chat. I can't do that. Can you? They can, and boy, will they ever.

One influence-peddler, who represents the association of for-profit hospitals and hospital corporations, said recently that "we have to be forceful. If you look at the gas people and the restaurant people, the people who yelled the loudest did the best." The gas people yelled about the BTU tax in the 1994 Clinton budget and killed it, while the restaurateurs protected tax deductions for entertainment. In case you were wondering just how crassly commercialized American medicine has become, the answer is, no more so than the gas or the restaurant business. And no less willing to try anything legal to nail a wayward senator to the wall.

The health industry giants pump enormous amounts of cash into the campaign coffers of those politicians they hope to befriend. Citizen Action, a consumer advocate group, found that the health and insurance industries have given a total of $153 million to congressional campaigns since 1979. This private tax on our health care system has been increasing rapidly, nearly quadrupling from just over $9 million for the 1980 elections to almost $34 million in 1992. Every dollar is money taken away from real health care. The Republican minority whip, Newt Gingrich of Georgia, received $429,374 over the thirteen years, and he was not the top recipient of health and insurance special interests' largesse. One lobbyist, referring to the coming health reform debate, told *Newsweek* in July 1993, "You have a $900 billion poker game that is about to start." What he didn't mention was how much you have to ante up before you're allowed to sit down at this high-stakes table. Your congressional representative may have a vote that's up for grabs, but you can't even afford to place a bet.

The special interests also take their misleading case to the public, in the form of slickly produced, enormously expensive ad campaigns—the kind of thing that the people who desperately need real reform cannot afford to fight against. Surgeons' public relations representatives liken their clients to symphony conductors, on stage for a brilliant performance in the operating theater. They don't remind you that there will be only one or two actual conductors in a large city who even approach *average* surgeons in income, while thousands of surgeons in the same city do unnecessary operations at ridiculously inflated prices. Drug makers tug at your heartstrings with stories of people kept alive and out of the hospital by their products. But they don't tell you that medical experts have judged their ads to be frequently misleading; or that the companies spend more on promotion of drugs—some with very dubious value—than they do on research; or that drug profits are rising several times faster than those of Fortune 500 companies generally.

The Prudential Insurance Company runs ads advocating more and more managed care, citing the importance of prevention. But they omit to mention that they, like other health insurance giants, have moved heavily into the managed care business themselves, with health plans enrolling paying patients in forty-five cities. And the members of the AMA, bless their hearts, try to convince you that cost controls in health care would lead to increased costs. This brilliant logic may convince the AMA membership, but the average American is going to think of the size of the more out-of-sight medical incomes. And the Association of Trial Lawyers of America, who reject out of hand any serious tort reform, try to get you to believe that the more lawyers and lawsuits we have, the better off we are.

What these ads do most effectively is to scare politicians, who know about the electoral weapons these groups have at their command: money, more money, and still more money. If they succeed in retarding reform, or in bending reform to their own financial advantage, these special interests will have completed the final step in the process by which American medicine's Golden Age degenerated into an Age of Gold.

But the strangest of all obstacles to change is us: we, the people. We, the ill, trembling with a frequently justified fear. We, the doting relatives of a dangerously ill or dying person, trying to stave off grief. We, the voters, who know we may become ill and want no expense to be spared, at least in our own case. We who, whatever else we may want, are very sure we do not want to die.

Save money on somebody else, sure. But us? Spare no expense, Doc. Anyway, heh, after all, uh, isn't somebody else paying? I mean, what have we got to lose? You think it might work? Try it. It's only experimental? So what? Look, I heard about it from a lady in my building. I think her husband had it. Like she said, nothing but the best. We've got to try it, Doc. It might work, right? We've got to try everything that has a chance to work.

Now, the patient or family member has nothing to lose, or so they think. The doctor on the other hand has quite a bit to gain: do the procedure, swell the volume, collect the reimbursement. It might work, and in any case the cash register is ringing.

The result is a collusion between doctor and patient, with the third-party payer standing by, paying the bill, and passing on the costs in the form of higher premiums or taxes. Unlike some collusions in the health care business, this one is not really evil. It is based on hope. Often the hope is unjustified, but it is almost always there. And it leads us to spend large sums of money, and sometimes to cause dreadful and useless pain, in a vain effort to stave off the inevitable. I call it the "what-if-it's-your-mother" principle, and its consequence is therapeutic relentlessness—a refusal to stop treatment until every technological trick has been tried, no matter what the pain or cost.

Increasingly, our hospitals are involved in salvage, and many people, especially the elderly, live in fear that when the time comes they will not be allowed to die in peace. In 1986 a 76-year-old woman got a liver transplant in Pittsburgh, and articles have appeared in leading medical journals with the titles "Open-Heart Surgery in Octogenarians" and "Outcomes of Surgery in Patients 90 Years of Age and Older." Some of this is valid, but such efforts could be extended without limit. If they are, we will never control costs, and we won't have the money to vaccinate or educate our children. As ethicist Daniel Callahan has pointed out, some limits have to be set. But most of us are not even willing to think about them.

THESE, THEN, ARE THE OBSTACLES to change, and they are large ones. Yet the American people have made abundantly clear, not only in polls but in referenda and elections too, that they want major change in their health care system. Republicans' hot air on the subject and their defense of the status quo clearly figured in their being turned out of the White House.

The Clinton administration has a mandate for change.

THE

CURE

So here is the scene: You are working alone in the emergency room. Our nation's health care is brought in on a stretcher, looking pale and feeble after a decades-long mugging. The patient's heart is in a dangerous abnormal rhythm. Next to the stretcher is a tray with useful tools and drugs. An executive at your side—maybe a hospital administrator, maybe an insurance company manager—is advising you to hold back. The hour is late, the patient's eyes are full of fearful expectation.

Doctor Clinton, what are you going to do?

Unquestionably, the Clintons have identified some of the major problems of our current system, but this is not difficult. Most of the problems are evident to anyone who has been sick, who had a sick family member, or who occasionally watches the evening news. Tragically, though, the Clintons may actually have fixed on the worst solution to this complex crisis. It is called "managed competition," although "mangled competition" would be a more apt name.

It was born whole out of the head of an obscure businessman-professor, more or less as Athena was born out of the head of Zeus—except that in the Greek story Zeus was a god, Athena was highly intelligent, and, in any case, the whole thing was a myth. As far as anyone understands the managed competition theory—and not many people do—it goes something like this. Under managed competition, all doctors and other caregivers will be under the administrative thumb of six or eight immense, for-profit insurance companies, which will have gobbled up hundreds of smaller insurers. Many, probably most doctors will actually work for these corporate giants, which are currently muscling into control of HMOs—increasingly just insurance businesses with doctors on salary. Others will stay "independent" (read *incredibly hassled and on a very short leash*), but be forced into PPOs—preferred provider organizations—which pay doctors a fixed amount per procedure done on a patient instead of a fixed salary.

Either way, your choice of doctor—or dentist, or psychotherapist, or nurse practitioner—will be drastically shrunk from what it is for most Americans now. HMOs restrict your choices to those doctors on *their* payroll. What? You don't care for any of the three gynecologists they have? You say one is too old and doesn't like your sex habits, the second doesn't have a minute to listen to your problems, and the third grinned in a way you didn't like when your feet were in the stirrups? Sorry, you should have thought of that when you joined up. All three are good doctors with clean records—save lots of money for the firm. Of course, you can always go elsewhere and pay for it out-of-pocket. But we can't help you there.

Surely, you say, PPOs must be better? Wrong again. PPOs are basically loosely organized HMOs. Money from your premiums goes to the insurance company bosses, who have a list of doctors you are allowed to consult. Having served on a committee at my university overseeing the transition from Blue Cross/Blue Shield to a PPO, I can tell you that the list is short—by design. A large number of people who wanted their own family doctors and specialists with whom they had relationships were left out in the cold. It wasn't that there was anything wrong with these excluded doctors; even the company didn't argue that. It was just that in order to keep profits up in today's environment the bean counters had to keep firm control of doctors, and that meant keeping the number of doctors low.

False claims about the superiority of HMO care have been circulating for years and are a centerpiece of Clinton propaganda for managed competition. But studies increasingly show that patients in these plans are very dissatisfied. A study published in the *Journal of the American Medical Association* on August 18, 1993, measured the ratings given by over 17,000 patients in three cities to three types of health care providers: small doctors' offices, large medical practices, and HMOs. Between 62 and 69 percent of the patients who saw doctors in small offices rated their care as excellent. For HMOs, excellent ratings ranged from 37 to 55 percent. "Patients bounce around in these systems," one of the researchers said. "It's the dark side of managed care." The director of the Harvard Community Health Plan, which (as I know from personal experience as well as national ratings) is one of the best HMOs in the country, admitted, "Large organizations can become impersonal quite easily."

Patients in HMOs feel shortchanged routinely. They wait a long time for a very short appointment. Patients of independent doctors were much more satisfied with their doctor's explanation of their illness and its treatment. Most important, they were more likely to feel that their doctor cared about their well-being. The main effect of the Clinton plan will be to collar vast numbers of Americans who now see independent doctors and herd them into HMOs, some of which will be like the ones these researchers studied but some of which will be far worse. And the satisfaction level of the average American who has to visit a doctor will take a very steep drop.

Jane Bryant Quinn, *Newsweek* consumer columnist, wrote a piece in September 1988 called "Forcing You Into an HMO." She predicted then that employers' outlook on health care would be "no more Mr. Nice Guy. Increasingly, you will find yourself lured, or kicked, into a health maintenance organization. Right now, HMOs are generally offered alongside a traditional plan, so employees can choose. In the future, that choice will be taken away." She must have had a crystal ball.

But I doubt whether she realized that five years later, almost to the day, a new president would announce a plan that would take that choice away from tens of millions of Americans in one fell swoop. Sure, in the managed competition maze it will theoretically be possible to find your way to an independent doctor. But it will be hard, and the difficulty will increase relentlessly as the years go by. Both the Bush and Clinton White Houses have consistently claimed that Americans would never put up with the long waits and short doctor visits common in some other countries, such as Britain and Japan (but not Canada or France, where no such problems exist). It is supremely ironic that the widespread dissatisfaction with HMOs in America today falls into exactly the same pattern. Managed competition will make that dissatisfaction universal. In fact, universal complaints are going to come much sooner than universal coverage.

It's not for nothing that the Clinton plan has been called "The Insurance Industry Preservation Act of 1993." That name is perfect, since the preservation of six or eight enormous insurance corporations is the only goal managed competition achieves that single payer does not. And far from giving us a desperately needed relief from bureaucracy, managed competition will add yet another layer of government bureaucracy, to watch the insurance company bureaucrats as they, in turn, watch the doctors. Think of it: *a whole new layer of bureaucracy*.

How can the Clinton administration have gotten this so wrong?

The short answer is that they backed into it under pressure from the Kerrey presidential campaign early in the 1992 primary season. Harris Wofford had won a hotly contested U.S. Senate seat against a Republican favorite son who had been a popular Pennsylvania governor, and he won it on one issue: health care. His stump speech argument was, if a criminal has a right to a lawyer, a law-abiding sick American should have a right to medical care. Bob Kerrey had shown an honest commitment to this issue for years and was making it the engine of his presidential run. Bill Clinton had never shown much interest in it, but now he had to—without sounding like a traditional Democrat and, above all, without evoking the dreaded "L" word. The Clinton campaign did not have time to study the health care crisis in general or managed competition in particular, but they needed a health plank in their platform and they hastily decided managed competition would be it. It looked like the sort of thing a New Democrat would be able to swallow since it proposed to save the poor without offending Big Business—indeed, while swelling corporate coffers quite nicely.

The long answer is more complex—although not as complex as managed competition itself, which makes the IRS rules and regulations look easy. Consider the three principal power brokers behind the Clinton proposal, the smug triumvirate of managed competition. Look for a moment at their personal histories. Understanding where they have come from and how they think throws light on why this plan is so bad.

The self-styled "father" of the plan is Alain Enthoven, a 62-year-old business school professor who writes and speaks as if he has all the answers. He comes by this habit honestly, since he has done it all his life, most notably as a Pentagon analytic "genius" in the entourage of 1960s Secretary of Defense Robert McNamara. (Deborah Shapley, a McNamara biographer, states that it was McNamara who invented the term "managed competition.") The young men around McNamara were known collectively as the "Whiz Kids" for their unsurpassed intellectual arrogance. And they were among the "best and brightest" who gave us the Vietnam War, one of our greatest modern national failures and one in which the blame for failure rests largely with those who thought intellectual analysis could substitute for values and even for experience. Enthoven, at thirty, impatiently faced down a group of white-haired generals who had laid their lives on the line time and again in a troubled century, and told them he hadn't come to listen to them but to tell them what he and his analysts had decided. He was not against the war by any means, just insistent on his own way of fighting it—from a comfortable Pentagon swivel chair.

The military did not enjoy Enthoven's arrogance. Leighton Davis, an Air Force general, echoed the sentiments of others in the officer corps when he said of Enthoven, "What's missing is the essence of military doctrine, ... judgment and operational factors. He didn't weight those very highly compared with the other quantifiable terms in his equations."

I would not belabor this history were it not for the fact that Enthoven's present approach to medicine and health is remarkably similar to his youthful approach to the disastrous Vietnam War. It is full of arcane equations and fine-sounding abstract theories, but devoid of experience, judgment, or sensitivity to the life-and-death realities at the other end of his computer. For example, in a classic and typical gaffe, during a petulant interview he gave the *New York Times Magazine* in July 1993, Enthoven said his benefits package would not cover vision care "other than treatment for eye injuries or inherited abnormalities." As pointed out by Dr. Scott Brodie, this would abandon almost every person with glaucoma, cataracts, diabetic retinopathy, and macular degeneration, four of the leading causes of blindness in America today. No doubt someone would have caught a blunder like Enthoven's before it became policy. Yet it shows how very far he is from the most elementary understanding of the real illnesses of real live patients.

Leaving the Pentagon in 1969, Enthoven took quick advantage of the government-business revolving door and became a vice president of Litton Industries, soon taking over Litton Medical Products as president. This work, far from patients and illness, was his only direct experience in the field of health; it lasted four years. But, true to form, he found it sufficient to form the basis for his abstract theories about how to transform America's health care system for the better. Enthoven's system would be comprehensive, it would be logical, it would be revolutionary, and above all it would get those irresponsible doctors under the thumb of sensible economists, just as he had done with the irresponsible generals at the Pentagon.

During the 1970s, as HMOs encroached relentlessly on the independence of doctors and the choices of patients, Enthoven was consulting for one of them (he still is) at very comfortable fees that nicely supplemented his business school income. He began inviting executives of the largest managed care corporations, along with top managers of commercial health insurers, to meet with him privately at the Jackson Hole, Wyoming, ski resort. He found that he shared with these corporate magnates both an enthusiasm for expensive winter sports and a desire to preserve a role for the growing commercial bureaucracy they managed. Oh yes, and they all relished their snobbish and adversarial stance against doctors. They kept on meeting as the insurance and managed care bureaucracy kept on growing, until some health reformers began to feel that the insurance industry was simply too powerful to be opposed any longer. Yet, according to Enthoven's own admission in a 1992 article in *Health Economics,* no consumer, labor, or senior citizen groups were included in these meetings.

Supposedly, Enthoven's great accomplishment at the Pentagon was that he rationalized procurement, a claim that in the early eighties was rendered laughable. Six-hundred-dollar toilet seats became the Rabelaisian emblem of where the Pentagon was tossing our hard-earned tax dollars.

But somehow bureaucratic memory was short enough that, by the nineties, Enthoven's new theories—no more than health care castles in the foggy academic air, clouded with financial conflicts of interest—were being taken seriously in Washington. This despite the fact that Enthoven was and is a highly paid consultant of a Kaiser managed care company, one of the nation's largest HMOs and among the most special of special interests, which stands to gain enormously if Enthoven's plan can be shoved through Congress; that over the years he has received over a million dollars in grants from foundations intimate with the health industry; and that for four years (at $10,000 a year, added to all his other health industry income) he was a director and stockholder of PCS, Inc., described in its parent company's annual report as a pharmaceutical managed care company "in a prime position to benefit from the rapid growth of managed care health plans." If the Clinton plan is passed, the father of managed competition can expect this brainchild to support him in his old age—and very nicely, thank you.

The second figure in the managed competition triumvirate is equally smug but even more shadowy. He is Ira Magaziner, the official head of President Clinton's Task Force on National Health Care Reform. Hillary Rodham Clinton's right-hand man, he was described by the *New York Times*—which supports his effort uncritically—as "an agitator turned consultant who now presides in the corridors of power." Radical back in the sixties, he spearheaded a successful drive to eliminate all course requirements at Brown University, making Brown notorious even today among educators who still believe in standards. After a stint at Oxford, he spent a couple of years trying to organize a food cooperative and a tenants' rights organization in the shoe-factory town of Brockton, Massachusetts. But, running out of activist steam, he apparently found which side his bread was likely to be buttered on. He turned himself into a consultant for major corporations like General Electric and Corning, eventually commanding $500 an hour or more for his advice, which, presumably, was no longer directed mainly toward helping the poor.

He built his own consulting firm and sold it in 1986 for an estimated $6 million, only to start another such firm in 1990. And he continued to toy with social engineering projects during this period. For example, he devised a vast, centralized industrial development plan for the state of Rhode Island; it was rejected by that state's voters overwhelmingly in a special referendum. One critic, a Brown University economist, called Magaziner's plan "absurd" and pointed to its favoritism toward certain companies. In 1989, Magaziner urgently advised the federal government to invest heavily in cold fusion, a scientific flash in the pan that is now merely an embarrassment to its former enthusiasts.

His qualifications for the job the Clintons gave him are in the realm of pure management and thought, devoid of medical experience or knowledge. The job is responsible for a system worth more than $900 billion a year, rapidly mounting toward a trillion. A former colleague with a favorable view of Magaziner gave this assessment of what he would accomplish: "Ira thinks in very broad strokes ... he will need nuts-and-bolts people to put his strategy into effect in the real world, at the level of the average person, because he thinks at a more global level." In other words, he is as abstract and detached as Professor Enthoven, and as a social engineer he has a long record of failure. The people who can "put his strategy into effect in the real world" have not yet been born; he has drawn a blueprint for a building that cannot stand.

But the most fascinating, most enigmatic, and most disappointing member of this troika is, of course, Hillary Rodham Clinton. A very talented lawyer, named among the nation's 100 best attorneys by her colleagues in the American Bar Association, she has devoted many years to a superb organization, the Children's Defense Fund, led by Marian Wright Edelman, serving it as a director and then chairing its board. The children of America have no better advocate than the CDF, and Mrs. Clinton deserves some of the credit for its success. She has made scholarly contributions to the law bearing on children's rights, and has fought alongside Edelman for prenatal care, parent education, child protection, and the like.

In fact, it can be unequivocally stated that if Hillary Rodham Clinton had been put in charge of children and families instead of health care on Inauguration Day, we would by now have had a superb plan for dramatically improving children's welfare. I for one would have been cheering loudly, and I have the receipts from my CDF contributions and my past writings on its work to prove it. It isn't as if children and families aren't also facing a crisis as serious as the current crisis in health care. An epidemic of physical and sexual abuse, teen pregnancy, violence in the schools, falling education standards, and even some health problems special to children—such as low vaccination rates and emergency room mishandling of the youngest patients—are not small or simple problems, and they are perhaps even more vital to the future of this nation than is health care. Mrs. Clinton is an undisputed expert in these critical areas, and no one except the extreme religious right could have gainsaid her credentials.

But the First Lady was put in charge of health reform. This proved tricky. No previous president had tried to give his wife so much power. Because she is the president's wife, she could be appointed without congressional approval, although her appointment clearly gave her more power than most Cabinet secretaries. Reams of journalistic commentary focused on this unique administrative gambit, distracting attention from the real issues of health. She then used (abused) her status as First Lady to try to conduct the business of health reform in secret. Mrs. Clinton claimed that she was not subject to the usual rules regarding openness of government advisory groups. Interested parties outside the government had to take the White House to court, a costly and wasteful diversion, to force Mrs. Clinton to bring the American people openly into a process that should have been open from the beginning. A lower court recognized the American people's right to look in on what she was doing and urged her out of secrecy. The U.S. Court of Appeals for the District of Columbia ruled in June 1993 that the secrecy was legal after all. But the result of Mrs. Clinton's steadfast resistance was a temporary but well-deserved loss of credibility.

During this same period she emerged as a self-assured moral crusader depicted by the *New York Times Magazine* in a scathing portrait as "Saint Hillary," a Joan of Arc figure "more preacher than politician," who wants to remake almost every aspect of American life. In a speech in Austin in April 1993, she directly insulted the American people, declaiming that we suffer from a "sleeping sickness of the soul" and need to be led out of "this spiritual vacuum." This is heady stuff, and potentially powerful in shaping her own and her husband's leadership on health and many other issues. Yet asked what she means by the catchphrase "politics of meaning," which she has used repeatedly, she confesses, "I don't have any coherent explanation ... I hope one day to be able to stop long enough to write down what I do mean ... because I have floated around the edges of this and talked about it for many, many years with a lot of people, but I've never ... really tried to get myself organized enough to do it." Her inability to explain this meaningless phrase is no indictment since its inventor, magazine editor and self-appointed national philosopher Michael Lerner, has never managed to explain it either.

But they are working on it: "As Michael Lerner and I discussed, we have to first create a language that would better communicate what we are trying to say, and the policies would flow from that language."

Thus she will solve Washington gridlock and American alienation by first, uh, creating a new philosophical language. As for Lerner's "practical" proposals for remaking America's ethics, his descriptions of them in his magazine, *Tikkun,* amount to nothing more nor less than a kind of psychobabble totalitarianism, designed to coerce the American people into caring and sharing. Lerner calls for constant government monitoring of virtually everything, and for endless reports in which almost all Americans would have to justify their activities according to his ethical mandate. That his vision is influencing Mrs. Clinton's health reform effort even indirectly is a frightening thought indeed.

"I want to be a voice for children in the White House," said Hillary Rodham Clinton during the campaign. What a loss to the kids of America (of whom I have three) that she was not made the "czar" of children's welfare. Instead, for some unknowable reason, she was put in charge of health reform, an area where she is a rank amateur. She has neither training nor experience in any medical field, in health economics or management, in health education, or even in health law. Until her father's unfortunate final illness last spring, she apparently did not even have experience with significant illness in her family. She has since referred frequently in her speeches to what she learned from her father's illness; clearly this was a powerful experience for her, and the nation genuinely sympathized. But in fact she remains less experienced than many Americans her age as a patient or patient's family member.

I don't care how quick a study she is, she can't master in a matter of months all the intricacies of medicine, health, prevention, distribution, payment, and law entailed in making even the most basic decisions about this problem. One seventh of the world's largest national economy, employing 11 million doctors, nurses, educators, therapists, and supporting staff, have hundreds of millions of patient encounters every year occasioned by thousands of diseases. Not even the most brilliant First Lady in history, which Mrs. Clinton may be, can learn what she has to know in the time she has allotted for it. Thus it is not surprising that a plan that was to be announced on May 1, 1993, was delayed until May 15, and then to June, July, and September. Still, the notion that she could get on top of these problems by convening hundreds of experts in secret to educate her requires a far stretch of the imagination.

Not surprisingly, the Task Force has given off a consistent air of bumbling and waffling, whether during its plenary sessions or after it was reduced to a skeleton structure in May. "Clinton Rules Out Delay in Unveiling Health Care Plan," blared a headline in April, "Economic Aides Rebuffed." But eventually the economic wizards won the delay they wanted, over Mrs. Clinton's vigorous protest. They wanted still more delays, because they were properly afraid of public reaction.

The administration has taken the wrong approach, with the wrong people, under the wrong leadership all along. It will continue to do so. If they think they had a hard time during the spring of 1993, that's nothing compared to the battle they face now that their plan has been unveiled. For months it was promised that the bill would be law by Christmas 1993. Now even the optimists are pointing to March 1, 1994, and others to much later dates.

I admire Mrs. Clinton. Without doubt she is the most remarkable First Lady since Eleanor Roosevelt redefined the office. But she has rushed down the wrong path on health care. She has run from the devil of "price-gouging" doctors and plunged into the deep blue sea of corporate health insurance and managed care, and now she is swimming with the sharks. Whether she will be eaten remains to be seen, but the indications are that she can avoid this fate only by becoming one of them.

But what of the plan itself? In early September, a draft *outline* for the legislation was leaked to the major media. It raised the possibility of a good benefits package; an "employer mandate," requiring employers to provide coverage for workers, with a subsidy available for companies with fewer than fifty workers; major cuts in Medicare and Medicaid; independent doctors only for those who can pay high premiums; and new taxes. On September 22, President Clinton made his long-awaited health care speech, which continued his and his wife's tradition of vagueness. "It was more of a pep talk than it was a detailed game plan," said NBC news anchorman Tom Brokaw after the speech ended. Even the printed outline of the plan was only a draft, and will change dramatically in Capitol Hill committees. The president proposes, but Congress disposes. Still, the plan at the outset has three major parts.

First, it recognizes the broad-stroke criticisms of the current system: 37 million uninsured (a steadily rising number), out-of-control costs, patient dumping, "cherry picking," high-tech bias, price gouging, and so on. These now amount to clichés; even Republicans and the AMA accept many of them. Being right about them has become easy, and can no longer win points for any specific reform proposal.

Second, it gives details of the coverage. However, these are all negotiable and are already being fought over in Congress. Among the questions for debate: Will there be co-payments or deductibles? Will there be a standard benefits package? Will dentistry, psychotherapy, or long-term care be included? Will there be budget ceilings? What will be the balance between prevention and cure, primary and specialized care? These are important questions, and God (or the Devil) is in the details. The details will be worked out in congressional committees, and because of the bill's wide ramifications many committees in both houses will get a crack at it. But there is nothing about the details of coverage that presupposes a particular way of organizing payment for health care, whether managed competition, single payer, or status quo.

Finally, there is the essence of the proposal: the organization of payment. This is the only part of managed competition that is distinctive, and therefore the one on which our evaluation of it must be based. And here it fails utterly, for six reasons.

One, it is merely an abstraction. Unlike single payer, or for that matter several other reform options, it has never been tried anywhere, and there is no reason to believe it would work.

Two, it largely destroys your free choice of doctor. If you belong to an HMO you have already had the experience of having to choose among only a few doctors, none of whom you like, or of giving up a doctor you may have relied on for years or decades. Under managed competition this experience will become almost universal.

Three, its main purpose is to preserve a role for a completely superfluous bureaucracy, the commercial insurers and their fellow travelers. As the CEO of a leading Canadian hospital said to me recently, "Your problem in the States is that you have a completely unproductive sector of the health economy, the insurance companies, and you seem to insist on preserving them at all costs."

Four, it is incomprehensible. The claim that it will give the average American control over medical care by enabling comparison of competing insurance plans presupposes a level of understanding of the system that is vanishingly unlikely. Ralph Nader has joked that to choose wisely among the alternatives offered you once a year, you will first have to go to graduate school.

Five, it invokes market forces to solve the problems of America's health care. Everyone from conservative former Surgeon General C. Everett Koop to liberal Princeton health economist Uwe Reinhart has concluded that market forces just don't work in the health sector. Demand is too elastic, and the temptation always to offer more, including unwarranted services, undermines cost reduction when market forces alone are relied on.

Six, the morale of physicians, perhaps the most precious element of any health care system, will be destroyed, perhaps forever. The burdens of paperwork and insolent telephone calls from bureaucrats are already driving doctors out of medicine and making them hate both their profession and their patients. Managed competition will increase these burdens, first by forcing independent doctors into managed care plans, then by adding a new layer of federal bureaucracy to supervise the plans. If you think you can get good care from doctors with low morale, you simply do not understand medicine.

Managed competition will perpetuate, even institutionalize, the vast waste of money that is spent on private health insurance. It is indeed ironic that Americans fear government bureaucracy so much that they are allowing themselves to be driven right into the nets of the biggest, most obnoxious, most useless bureaucracy of all—that of the largest commercial health insurance corporations. The six or eight largest of these will eat up all the smaller fry and then will permanently administer a corporate oligopoly unresponsive to anyone's needs but their own.

In addition, under managed competition, full coverage of the uninsured will be delayed for years—even the optimistic President Clinton says five to seven years—and, according to our own government reports, cost control may very well fail. Thus the two central goals that, by universal agreement, must be attained by any health reform will not be achieved by the Clinton plan in the foreseeable future. It is so needlessly complex, so confusing, so ignorant of real health issues, and so stubbornly reliant on market forces that will not work, that it really does deserve the name "mangled competition." It resembles nothing so much as a Rube Goldberg machine, which operated by, say, having a monkey pull a chain, dumping water on a cat, who screeched, waking a night watchman, whose startled head pushed a button, which activated a series of gears and levers the last of which lobbed a ball into a basketball hoop, which turned on a gas flame, which burned through a string, which released a switch, which activated some gears, which … well, you get the idea. At the end of these farcical sequences, Goldberg, an engineer-turned-cartoonist, would have the apparatus serve its ultimate purpose—something like switching on a light bulb. "Why not simplify health reform?" Dr. Steffie Woolhandler, a leading advocate of a Canadian-style plan, asked on June 24, 1993, in *USA Today*. Why not, indeed?

Mrs. Clinton's strategy from the beginning was evidently to declare war on doctors, the easiest target. Patients encounter and know them but not the faceless insurance company bureaucrats who are the worst villains of the system. Doctors deserve their share of blame, but they are not the enemy. They are the officer corps of our own health care army. Their morale is so low you can barely find it anymore. They are overwhelmed with insults and bureaucratic hassles, especially from commercial insurers. True, some doctors are greedy. But most are making moderate incomes working hours that few of us would tolerate, shouldering enormous responsibility, and doing the hardest job in the world, and the one that requires the longest and most arduous training. No one challenges their intelligence and skill, which are universally admired.

Yet they have proved easy scapegoats for the Clintons, who want to emphasize their greed as the system's greatest villainy. Not the greed of insurance company directors, who are swallowing the health care system whole to feed their profit motive. Not the greed of drug company CEOs, who can make up to $13 million a year. Not the greed of hospital investors, who slam the door in sick people's faces. Not the greed of ambulance-chasing lawyers, who make a mockery of justice while making a fast buck. Not the greed of senators, congressional representatives, and presidential candidates, who palm campaign cash offered to them by the health moguls as if electoral contributions were going out of style. But first, foremost, and only, the greed of practicing doctors, the only special interest group that actually takes care of the sick; the only group among the major players that irrevocably belongs in the health system.

Not only did President Clinton *consult* top soldiers about force in Bosnia and gays in the military, but he ended up following the advice of military professionals on both issues. Where were the liberal leaders of American medicine and public health when the Clinton health care task force was convened with virtually no caregivers on it? I'm not talking about the profit-hungry doctors who dominate the AMA. I'm talking about dedicated, selfless women and men who badly want real change. Oh yes, I forgot! They are an interest group, like commercial insurers and malpractice lawyers! Except for one detail: most major industrial democracies have jettisoned two of these three interest groups from health care and have systems better than ours; none has yet found a way to eliminate doctors.

The dominant advisers in the task force were insurance company executives. There was a photo in the *New York Times* under the title, "Hillary Clinton's Potent Brain Trust On Health Reform." All in the photo were middle-aged white males. Of the ten named, four were insurance company executives, two more were from Pepsico and General Electric, and one was from the Pharmaceutical Manufacturers Association. Most of these consultants are corporate fat cats making money hand over fist from the disaster of our health care system. Some brain trust. It should have been called the profits trust. No wonder they tried to hold their meetings in secret. Patient choice and physician morale were the two lowest items on their agenda. The people Mrs. Clinton consulted most actively are the same people other countries have simply kicked out of health care—with excellent results.

The Clinton plan also preserves and expands the link between employment and health care, which most of the industrialized world has greatly reduced or jettisoned. The employer mandate, requiring all businesses to cover their employees, is a centerpiece of the plan, and, despite talk of a subsidy, it will devastate small business. According to John Motley, vice president of the National Federation of Independent Businesses, the smallest businesses, frequently minority-owned, will be hit the hardest, and job creation will suffer: "Small business is labor intensive, that's why we create jobs." Various studies estimate a loss of 400,000 to 1.5 million jobs just during the first year of the employer mandate. Payroll taxes, which may have to be raised to fund the Clinton plan, would cause further job loss.

Meanwhile, those who are working would continue to have their coverage dependent on their role as employees. Job lock would continue, since the guaranteed coverage for the unemployed would be a second-rate type of care and, in any case, would not be phased in for years. Early retirees aged fifty-five to sixty-five (some 4 million people, many retired against their will) would, because of the employment link, have to be covered by an entirely new mechanism. No one, not even the plan's keenest admirers, claims that managed competition could be made to work in rural America. That vast sector of our nation will simply have to be covered in some other way, because population density is too low to sustain the Byzantine apparatus of purchasing pools that the Clinton plan requires. Finally, it is likely that some of America's largest corporations would be exempted from participating in the health insurance pools as required of everyone else. They would then be in full control of their employees' medical options—an authoritarian situation if there ever was one.

Politically, managed competition can, should, and will fail. It is being opposed by Republicans; conservative Democrats afraid of going down with the Clintons; the AMA because it will indirectly limit fees; the drug firms because it will try to end their price gouging; the small business associations because the employer mandate will force many thousands of their members into bankruptcy; small insurance companies because hundreds will be abolished; and all the consumer and labor organizations that favor the single payer option.

The name Clinton has become more synonymous with bungling than that of any president since Gerald Ford, and that minority of the voters who put him in office is, if we can believe the polls, not holding firm. With his economic recovery stalled, his budget eviscerated in committee, his foreign policy a shambles, his White House a morass of ethical tangles and personal disaster, and his down-home Arkansas image lost in a cloud of $200 coiffed hair, Clinton is not someone any sensible Democrat in Congress with the slightest political vulnerability would want to tie his or her fortunes to. Certainly he could recover (although no modern president has ever had this low an ebb of approval to recover from), but barring a miracle he cannot recover soon enough to put a distrusted, totally baffling, and basically bad proposal through Congress this year or, probably, next.

ALTHOUGH WHAT THE CLINTONS PROPOSE to do will not solve our major problems, there is a solution under discussion in Congress. It's the American Health Security Act of 1993, introduced by Senator

Paul Wellstone of Minnesota. It is cosigned by senators Daniel Inouye, Carol Moseley-Braun, Howard Metzenbaum, and Paul Simon. Representative Jim McDermott has introduced a similar bill in the House with eighty-seven cosponsors—and the bill is just getting off the ground. This is real reform, not the minor tinkering that the Clintons are doing under the supervisory eye of the insurance companies. It learns from, but does not mimic, the Canadian plan, a single payer system administered at the state level. It is, as the Clintons like to claim for their own plan, an American solution to an American problem.

But unlike the Clinton plan, it does not have insurance industry preservation as a central goal, nor does it stubbornly reject everything tried and proven north of the border. It leaves patients free to choose, while controlling costs and covering everyone. Most important, it takes the insurance companies out of the decision-making loop, freeing doctors to do what they love best: doctoring. Paradoxically, doctors will have far more independence under the Wellstone bill than under the Clinton reforms. The Wellstone bill is real reform. If we don't pay attention to it now, we'll simply be forced to after the Clinton reforms fail.

The advantages of single payer read like a wish list for the health care system that we need. Here are a few:

- *Universal coverage.* Every American, regardless of age, sex, race, or economic status, will have health insurance, just by virtue of being an American. Period.

- *Full, free choice of doctor.* Every American will be able to go to any doctor or legally recognized health professional in the nation. Period.

- *Basic benefits guaranteed.* A nationally mandated standard benefits package will ensure specific coverage in all vital areas, including substantial coverage for preventive measures, long-term care, home care, and mental health.

- *Independent doctors.* Doctors and other caregivers will *not* work for the government; bean counters and paper pushers will— except for those who will have to look for new work outside the health care system.

- *No link to employment.* Your coverage will in no way depend on your job, which puts an end to paralyzing "job lock" and to employers' unfair leverage over your life.

- *Hassle-free payment.* Your caregiver will have no difficulty or delay in collecting a legitimate fee, and you will not be involved. There will be no forms to fill out and no haggling with insurance companies over reimbursement.

- *Care maps.* You and your doctor will have scientific guidelines that strongly suggest paths and limits of care; for the first time, you will be protected from unwarranted overtreatment.

What would your life be like under a single payer system?

You would carry a card identifying you as a legitimate recipient of health care. When you needed to see a doctor, you would choose any doctor you wanted. At the doctor's office your card would be run through a machine much like a credit card machine. You would get the care you needed from the doctor of your choice. The form stamped with your card would be sent by the doctor's office to the agency assigned by the state legislature to be the single payer in your state. The doctor would be paid promptly and usually without question. The state-level agency would monitor doctors for strange patterns of use, set fees and budget ceilings, and regulate the number of hospital beds, coronary bypass units, magnetic resonance imagers, and the like. Doctors would be completely independent except for this one layer of supervision. They could organize their practices in any way they chose—except for such antics as self-referral, doing needless procedures, and taking unfair profits. Insurance-business profits would become a thing of the past. Administrative costs in the system as a whole would be somewhere between six and nine cents on the dollar. At least 90 percent of every health care dollar would go directly for the care of the sick.

There are many possibilities for financing single payer, but none of them would cost the average American more money. If you have insurance, your deduction for your premium, as well as your employer's contribution to the insurer on your behalf, would no longer be made. Under the Wellstone bill's proposal, these payments would be replaced by a 7.9 percent payroll tax on employers, an expansion of the 1.45 percent tax now paid for Medicare; an increase in corporate income tax from 34 to 38 percent, for businesses with over $75,000 in profits; and a 2 to 3 percent hike in the income tax in the middle and higher brackets. These seem like big increases, but don't forget there will be no more payments to for-profit commercial insurers. The vast majority of currently insured people will experience no significant change in what they pay for health care.

Many Americans, especially health professionals, are concerned that a single payer system would have all the drawbacks of Medicare and Medicaid. They correctly note that these government programs do not work efficiently or well. However, many of their problems stem directly from the fact that they must compete on an uneven playing field with for-profit insurers. The Profits Pact formed in the 1950s between the AMA and commercial insurers allows doctors to favor privately insured patients and, in turn, to be favored by the companies that insure them. Without these commercial forces a government payment system could generate top-quality care much more efficiently. Doctors also point out that the people currently in the government-payer bureaucracies are poorly trained. This could be solved by bringing some of the best middle-management people in the commercial health insurance industry into government. With a little willpower, and the help of middle-management professionals previously employed by commercial insurers, America could build a fine civil service for health care payment, just as every other advanced country has done.

Misconceptions and outright lies about the single payer option abound, a virtual disinformation campaign conducted by corporate interests in health and now by the Clinton White House. Here are some of them, along with the corresponding facts.

The single payer approach is socialized medicine.
False. Canadian medicine is independent and private, far more so than American medicine would be under managed competition. Only payment is run by the government, eliminating the wasteful, obstructive, for-profit insurance bureaucracy.

Single payer resembles the British system, with all its flaws.
False. The Canadian and British systems have very little in common, other than universal coverage and an elimination of corporate waste in the payment process. Canadians have complete and open choice of doctor, spend 50 percent more per capita than the British to get more, more timely, and higher-quality care, leave doctors independent instead of making them government employees, and have much higher levels of patient satisfaction than the British. Canadians can opt to buy private care out-of-pocket—going to the U.S. or to the handful of Canadian doctors who opt out of the system and set their own higher prices—but because of high levels of satisfaction with the system, few choose to do so.

Single payer leads to years-long waiting lists.
False. This is a myth of the managed competition propaganda campaign. Waiting lists in Canada are nonexistent for urgent care and reasonable for other care. HMO patients in the U.S. already have annoying waiting lists, and these will worsen drastically under the Clinton plan. Yet waiting lists here will be for further enhancement of HMO profits, while in Canada they exist only to serve the patient's interest. Because of America's massive overtreatment problem, we could actually benefit from the Canadian type of waiting list. If I had only equivocal indications for a coronary bypass—as do tens of thousands of Americans who get a bypass every year—I would be

happy to be put on a waiting list. My doctor would then give me a regimen of diet, exercise, and stress reduction, possibly augmented by drug treatment. With luck, by the time my name came up on the list, I might not need the surgery at all. That's not a delaying tactic, it's just good medicine. If I were unlucky and at some point needed surgery immediately, that's when I would get it: immediately.

Canadians constantly cross the border to see American doctors.

False. Despite aggressive marketing to Canadians by American hospitals close to Canada, border crossing is minimal. The American Medical Association surveyed administrators in nine border hospitals and found that fewer than 1 percent of the patients admitted to each of those hospitals were Canadians. The Pepper Commission, in its 1990 final report, found a maximum of 3 percent Canadian admissions to Buffalo General Hospital, with other border hospitals reporting even lower percentages. In one survey done by the Harris organization, 97 percent of Canadians said they would not trade their health care system for ours, while 61 percent of Americans said they would prefer the Canadian system to our own.

Canada has a cost-control crisis as bad as ours.

False. Not as bad as ours by a long shot. They have suffered cost increases (as has every health care system in the industrialized world). This is because of medical advances, an aging population, inflationary pressures on doctors' income caused by the proximity of the United States (doctors are the highest paid professionals in Canada), and a steady attempt to improve care for the disadvantaged. American critics of Canada's system call it to task for being behind the U.S. frontier of technology, and then turn around and point to cost control problems when Canada catches up. This makes no sense whatever. But the fact is that Canada will never have the kind of cost control problem we have. President Clinton himself, in his speech to the National Governors' Association on August 16, 1993, estimated that in the year 2000 Canada's costs will have gone up to 10 percent of gross domestic product, while ours, under current trends, will be at 19 percent.

Canada can't afford research and technological advances.

False. For a small country of 26 million people, Canada has a remarkable record of medical research. Insulin was discovered at the University of Toronto in 1921; the first pacemaker developed at Toronto General Hospital in 1950; the world's first coronary care unit established at Toronto General in 1962; and the powerful cancer drug vinblastine isolated from the periwinkle plant at the University of Western Ontario in 1956. Recently, Canadian researchers have located, identified, or sequenced the genes for muscular dystrophy, cystic fibrosis, and the T-cell receptor important in AIDS. Research could and should be better funded, but it is very far from backward. As for expensive high-tech equipment for diagnosis and treatment, it is distributed and used rationally, without the duplication and overuse that has become routine in the United States.

Doctors are deeply dissatisfied in Canada.

False. Initially, Canadian doctors opposed reform. Today the Canadian Medical Association officially supports the system. A 1992 survey done by *Physician's Management*, an American medical magazine, showed that 84 percent of Canadian doctors (as well as 90 percent of Canadian consumers) rated the quality of care in Canada as "good to excellent." Physician satisfaction in America is widely expected to go down under managed competition. Yet a study published in the *New England Journal of Medicine* showed that despite earning less money, Canadian doctors have higher levels of satisfaction than American doctors even today.

ONE OF THE MOST FREQUENT and most legitimate questions raised about the Clinton plan is, "How will it be paid for?" The federal government's own Health Care Financing Administration estimated in early May 1993 that it would cost an additional $100 to $150 billion to implement it. Even Ira Magaziner, the plan's dreamy designer, conceded that it could cost as much as $90 billion, but he and his secret committee figure that cost savings will offset some of this. Yet the May 1993 Congressional Budget Office (CBO) report on managed competition questions whether the plan will work to control costs at all. Thus the American people will be faced with a large new tax levy, and arguments will rage as to whether the money should come from tobacco and alcohol taxes, a value-added tax, a reduced tax break for health insurance, a payroll tax, or a tax on hospitals and doctors. President Clinton's own top economic advisers are publicly worried about the cost of his and his wife's plan.

The single payer answer is: No problem. There is no large new cost and no need for a new tax other than what we are already paying into insurance company coffers. The funds for the uninsured will come from tremendous administrative savings and from reduction of the enormous number of useless and unwarranted medical and surgical procedures. An April 1993 Congressional Budget Staff Memorandum (actually a fifty-page document) on the cost of single payer solutions reviewed four serious estimates of the change in national health expenditures under a single payer system. The estimates range from an 8 percent decrease, provided by Physicians for a National Health Program, to a whopping 5 percent increase, given by the CBO itself. The General Accounting Office's 1991 report, *Canadian Health Insurance: Lessons for the United States*, projected a decrease of 0.4 percent, and an independent research group publishing in *Health Affairs* foresaw a 4.2 percent increase. All these projections were made under the assumption that we cover *all* the uninsured and continue providing *all* the same services we provide now, except for useless procedures and useless pencil pushing. The CBO memorandum states that "the conservative assumption underlying the CBO's estimate may overstate spending." In other words, they admit the increase could be less than their 5 percent projection. Yet even if the cost increase is that high, it will only be $45 billion, less than half the projected cost increase under managed competition as estimated by the government's own Health Care Financing Administration.

And by the way: one of the most underhanded tricks used by opponents of single payer is to criticize the access and benefits in other countries without ever mentioning the fact that those countries spend much less on health care than we do. The question is not what single payer will do under the assumption of expenditures at 6 percent or 9 percent of gross domestic product (GDP), but what it will do at 14 percent, which is where we are now. Indeed, we could actually reduce our percentage of GDP spent on health care and still avoid dreaded waiting lists or reduced contact time with physicians.

Canada does not have long waiting lists for legitimate treatments or any sort of systematic undertreatment problem, nor does France, Holland, or Germany. As Richard Saltman, a health management expert at the Emory University School of Public Health, has shown in comparative studies, all these countries, with systems closer to Canada's than to ours, have health care delivery superior to ours. Britain, on the other hand, does not. Why? Because it only spends 6.5 percent of GDP on health care. Its problems come from that, not from the fact that it has a National Health Service instead of the chaos that we have. The other countries mentioned spend 8 or 9 percent. All could do better; improvement is always possible and will occur in all these countries with gradual, wise, controlled expenditure increases for research and new technology. They will never have our waste or our overtreatment problem because they have organized their health care systems rationally, mostly through the single payer approach.

Some would have you think that the single payer solution is the province of radicals and dreamers. Don't believe it. Despite great pressure to fall in line with a weakening president, six Democratic senators (including seasoned veteran Howard Metzenbaum and courageous newcomer Carol Moseley-Braun) and some eighty-nine congressional representatives (the total is steadily rising) have supported one or another single payer reform bill. So have grass roots groups like Consumers Union, Public Citizen, and Citizen Action; professional groups like the American Public Health Association, the National Association of Social Workers, and the American Medical

Student Association—so much for *their* supposed greed; ecumenical church groups like the Interreligious Council on Health Reform; and labor organizations from the Screen Actors Guild and Actors' Equity to the Ladies' Garment Workers and the Teamsters. Similar reforms are supported by at least 5,000 physicians who belong to Physicians for a National Health Program.

Ralph Nader, the man who said twenty-five years ago what everyone now believes about auto safety—including every executive in Detroit who once thought Nader a fool—supports the single payer approach to health reform. The 5,000 doctors who have joined a fledgling, poor, powerless club called Physicians for a National Health Program, paying a membership fee of $120 that buys nothing except the satisfaction of doing the right thing, represent tens of thousands more who are by nature nonjoiners but who think the same way. Many more doctors and other caregivers will join as it dawns on them that Canadian health professionals have far more independence, and fewer hassles, than they will have in America under managed competition, or even than many have today.

Consumer Reports, the magazine that for generations has been synonymous with the best interest of American consumers, has supported single payer since September 1991. The *New England Journal of Medicine*, arguably the world's most prestigious medical journal—the voice of the scientific and intellectual elite of the medical profession—came out in favor of a Canadian-style system on June 17, 1993. The June 1993 *Money* magazine, not exactly a socialist rag (the same issue had an article on "Top Blue-Chip Funds"), endorsed the Canadian plan outright. The *New Yorker* came out in favor of single payer on April 26, 1993, as did the *Atlanta Journal-Constitution* on September 11, 1993. There is a constantly growing ground swell of support for the single payer alternative.

Most important of all, polls have repeatedly shown that a comfortable majority of the American people—59 percent in a *New York Times*/CBS poll at the end of March—would like to have a health care system resembling Canada's. Sixty-one percent preferred the

Canadian system in a Louis Harris poll in 1988, 66 percent in a *Los Angeles Times* poll in 1990. These are not significant differences, just a consistent majority. There must be some kind of massive whisper campaign going on among ordinary folks, because the major media and the White House alike have done everything possible to stifle interest in single payer solutions. Congress and some of the media are now on the move in the right direction, but the American people are way ahead of them.

You might expect the forces of corporate insurance and corporate medicine, along with their academic apologists, to be worried about this growing support for the single payer option. They are. In the journal *Health Economics*, Enthoven and his colleagues wrote in 1992, "Hyperinflation in U.S. health services without commensurate increases in value is leading critics to demand increasing public intervention ... and elimination of a multiple-payer, private insurance industry. ... At issue is whether this transition can be achieved quickly enough, and whether it will be sufficient to forestall massive public intervention into the U.S. health care system." In other words, we'd better get managed competition passed, fellas, or we'll lose the ranch to these damn sheep farmers who don't appreciate profits.

What Enthoven and others like him miss, and have always missed, is that health care delivery is a public good, and its guardianship a public trust. The "sickness business" has violated that trust, and should return the system to the people of this country, so that they may try their own hand at guarding it.

One of the most disturbing questions I get from interviewers and audiences alike is, "Do you really think that the public will and the public good can prevail against the special-interest lobbyists in Washington?" I reply, "You are asking me if I believe in the American democracy," and we both have a good chuckle. But I do believe in the American democracy. Don't you? The questioners are not hopeless cynics, just decent people exhausted by betrayals of their trust, people who have come to doubt the ability of government to respond to their needs even a little.

All of us in what might be thought of as leadership positions—whether doctors, nurses, therapists, health administrators, insurance executives, journalists, clergy, teachers, lawyers, government officials, or legislators—must begin to act in such a way as to restore their trust. For once, forget the special interests, including your own. Let them take a back seat for a little while to the interests of the nation. I do not rejoice in President Clinton's string of losses and Pyrrhic victories; I voted for him with a certain enthusiasm and would probably do so again, especially if the only serious alternative was again an out-of-touch Republican. But health reform is far more important to this nation than his or anyone's political fortunes.

Aneurin Bevan, the brilliant public servant who led the drive to establish the National Health Service in Britain—he had been a miner at age thirteen but rose to become Minister of Health—said in 1948, "No society can legitimately call itself civilized if a sick person is denied aid because of lack of means." We, by this criterion, are not even close to being civilized.

I don't ignore the sacrifices that must be made by professionals who have devoted themselves to the cause of health. Many of these people are my friends, and I talk to them frequently in public and in private. To the physicians, I say: You are the field officers of the health care army. Stop bringing up the rear. Cut your ties to the minority among you who seek to profit from the misfortune of illness. Insist upon your expertise in how to fight its ravages. Reach back to American medicine's Golden Age, when reverence for your commitment was simply taken for granted, and few if any dreamed of accusing you of greed. Above all, fight the tragic public perception that you are part of the health establishment's faceless power elite. Let the blame for greed rest where it belongs: with the corporate entities that have largely conquered medicine and made your careers a mockery of what you once hoped they would be. Take the highest road. Oppose the Clintons from the single payer platform, and do it before it is too late.

To those who are employed by commercial health insurers, I could be flippant and suggest that you form a support group with former submarine factory executives and managers of erstwhile military bases. Or, I could suggest that you learn how to vaccinate children or track down pregnant teenagers with no prenatal care. But in fact I believe that there is a role for many of you in a single payer system, doing what you do best, helping to effect a very difficult transition, and serving state and local governments in many new and critical roles. America needs a more professional civil service if it is to administer a single payer system effectively. It needs your help.

To patients—and sooner or later that means every one of us—I say: We must face our own responsibilities. Don't expect miracles. Get over the wasteful fix-it mentality. Take prevention and compliance seriously. Stop blaming doctors for every natural accident. Sympathize with their frailty; they are only human. And most important, face the fact that we cannot afford to try everything that might work for every person who is ill. We already have rationing, but we do it in a way that is haphazard and unjust. We must do it according to the proven methods, for those who can really benefit. In the words of Ecclesiastes, there is a time to be born and a time to die. Sooner or later each of us must learn to let go.

What counts most in the meantime are not the niceties of policy, nor even our agreed-upon abstract ethical principles, but faces: the faces of the uninsured, sitting in pain hour after hour in emergency ward waiting rooms not far from our homes; of parents who worked and paid their premiums for years, dropped from coverage because their child has become chronically ill; of women who cannot afford routine gynecological care; of men denied insurance because they are florists or hairdressers; of middle-class families who must spend their life savings to zero before they can qualify for the assistance of their community when faced with a catastrophic illness.

What is it that we value most about the American democracy: rugged individualism, or a sense of fair play? If, as I hope and trust, it is the latter, then we need real health reform and we need it now. We say that we love and fight for freedom; but no person is free who must face disabling illness and pain without help and without resources.

We hear again and again the claim that single payer systems are *politically unacceptable.* Once, the progressive income tax was politically unacceptable. Social Security, integration of the armed forces, Medicare, voting rights—all politically unacceptable. If we let the most timid among us blaze our paths to the future, we would still be lost in a nineteenth-century jungle, trying to find a clearing for child labor laws and the regulation of slaughterhouses. We must stop thinking about what can get through the Congress right now, and think instead about what health care system will best serve this nation as we turn the corner of the millennium.

We need to aim much higher than the Clintons are aiming now. They want so much to be centrist, to avoid the so-called (and so far nonexistent) leftward lurch. Yet the question is not whether socialism is dead, but "How high will we build the floor under the poor?" Not whether a furnace of greed must burn in the economic house—all agree that it must—but whether those who live in the house can rely on each other at all.

The current health care crisis is a major illness. Managed competition is aspirin and a Band-Aid. When America calls in the morning it will be more fundamentally ill and in even greater pain. It urgently needs a more sensible, serious, and informed intervention— not the minor tinkering of managed competition, tinkering that leaves the greatest inequities and waste of our present system virtually intact. In Canada, *payment* is government-regulated; *medicine* is private, doctors independent, and patients free to choose. We've heard that the Canadian plan would give us the compassion of the IRS and the efficiency of the post office. More likely, it would be the prices of the post office and the efficiency of Norman Schwarzkopf's army—good enough for government work or any other sort of work. As for compassion, it would be hard for us to do worse than we do now.

Too many Americans are still fighting the war against socialism. We won that one, and should be proud. But the race now is not against Russia and Czechoslovakia, it is against the likes of Japan and Germany. They are the world's most vigorous capitalist economies, yet they hew to no rigid ideology about it. Where the market does the most effective job, they let the market do it. Where government intervention has a useful role to play, they use it, without standing on market-values ceremony. In the economic sphere, their only ideology appears to be success, and the only question is, "What works?" In health care, in both countries, government plays a large and salutary role. Their systems differ from Canada's, but they differ much more from ours, and from what ours would be like in the Rube Goldberg machine known as managed competition, a system that will take away our choices and in which cost control will amount to squeezing balloons. We do not have to think that single payer would be perfect to think that it would do better than that. And by the way, if the post office had the same efficiency as our present health care system, 37 million of us would never get any mail, and 60 million would only get it sometimes.

There are many details to be worked out, but our general direction for the future should be clear: not more bureaucrats, but more nurses and primary care doctors; not more magnetic resonance scanners, but more neighborhood clinics; not more angioplasties, but more vaccinations; not more burdens on caregivers, but fewer and more meaningful ones; not more wealth for commercial insurers, but a simple elimination of them; not more profits, but more humane care. Health care must surely take this general direction regardless of the details of its organization. But a careful attention to the details needed to bring about these changes, and to the much greater successes other countries have had in health, shows that the single payer path is by far the best way there.

Our nation is at a watershed in its social history. Not just our health and our dollars but our sense of fair play, tolerance, and community are at stake. The time has come to think about how our children will remember us—to stop dawdling and dickering and do the right thing. We are not so confused that we do not know what the right thing is. The only real question is, do we have the courage to do it?

Senator _____
United States Senate
Washington, D.C. 20510

OR

Representative _____
United States House of Representatives
Washington, D.C. 20515

Dear Senator _____ (or Representative _____):

I strongly support the single payer solution to America's health care crisis.
It is sometimes called "the Canadian plan," but there is a thoroughly
American version: the American Health Security Act of 1993, introduced
by Senator Paul Wellstone. (Representative Jim McDermott has a similar
bill in the House.) It is supported by at least ninety of your Senate and
House colleagues, including Carol Moseley-Braun, Daniel Inouye, and
Pete Stark, as well as Consumers Union, Citizen Action, leading labor
unions, *Money* magazine, and the *New England Journal of Medicine*. Even
President Clinton concedes its cost-efficiency.

But what the president doesn't say is more important. His own "mangled"
competition plan will cost more, create tremendous windfall profits for a
cabal of insurance-business behemoths, add a whole new layer of bureaucracy, destroy many thousands of small businesses, and take away our free
choice of doctor. The Clinton plan has aptly been called "The Insurance
Industry Preservation Act of 1993," since its most important result will be
to preserve and enhance this outmoded industry.

Please support the Wellstone-McDermott legislation, which is better in
every way. Don't let Big Business dictate the terms of health reform.
Don't let the giant insurance companies force me into their HMOs.
Prove that the democratic process is still more powerful than the special
interests. Instead of preserving the Illness Industry's profits, preserve my
free choice of doctor. Defeat the Clinton plan and replace it with real
health reform—the American Health Security Act of 1993.

Sincerely,

Notes

INTRODUCTION

p. 4: "Polls have already proven him wrong": The Gallup organization found in March 1993 that 65 percent of Americans are "very concerned" about the freedom to choose their own doctor. The same poll showed that 75 percent are "very concerned" about the plight of the uninsured, up from *five* percent in October 1990, and that 61 percent are "very concerned" about the quality of their own health care. Colburn, Don. "Health Care, Uninsured, Concern Americans." *Washington Post,* April 13, 1993. **p. 5:** "claiming that it 'would require us to replace…' ": President Clinton, addressing the National Governors' Association, August 16, 1993; as televised on C-SPAN.

THE CRISIS

p. 13: "American medicine's Golden Age": Burnham, John C. "American Medicine's Golden Age: What Happened to It?" *Science 215:*1474–9, 1982. **p. 13:** "Medical miracles": Beeson, Paul. "Changes in Medical Therapy During the Past Half Century." *Medicine 59:*79–99, 1980. **p. 13:** "Trust between doctor and patient has broken down": Johnson, G. Timothy. "Restoring Trust Between Patient and Doctor." *New England Journal of Medicine 322:*195–7, 1990. See also Burnham, John C., 1982. "American Medicine's Golden Age." **p. 13:** "Medical gurus": Siegel, Bernie. *Love, Medicine, and Miracles.* New York: Harper & Row, 1986; for a critique of Siegel and others like him, see Konner, Melvin. "Laughter and Hope." *New York Times Magazine,* March 13, 1988, pp. 49–50. **p. 14:** "the amount Americans now spend for 'alternative healing' ": Eisenberg, D. and five other authors. "Unconventional Medicine in the United States: Prevalence, Cost, and Patterns of Use." *New England Journal of Medicine 328:*246–53, 1993; and Murray, Raymond H. and Rubel, Arthur J. "Physicians and Healers: Unwitting Partners in Healing." *New England Journal of Medicine 326:*61–4, 1992; and Cassileth, Barrie R., Lusk, Edward J., Strouse, Thomas B., and Bodenheimer, Brenda J. "Contemporary Unorthodox Treatments in Cancer Medicine: A Study of Patients, Treatments, and Practitioners." *Annals of Internal Medicine 101:*105–12, 1984. **p. 14:** "people resent…doctors' inflated incomes": Hilts, Philip J. "Doctors' Pay Resented, and It's Underestimated." *New York Times,* March 31, 1993, p. A9. **p. 14:** "away from primary care": Colwill, Jack M. "Where Have All the Primary Care Applicants Gone?" *New England Journal of Medicine 326:*387–93, 1992; with accompanying editorial by Robert G. Petersdorf, pp. 408–9. For the corresponding information about Britain, see Allsop, Judy. *Health Policy and the National Health Service.* London: Longman, 1984 (a history, with a collection of relevant historical documents); and Hart, Julian Tudor. *A New Kind of Doctor: The General Practitioner's Part in the Health of the Community.* London: Merlin Press, 1988.

p. 14: "a collegial bond": Hart, Julian Tudor. *A New Kind of Doctor.* **p. 15:** "litigation…compensates few of the wronged patients": Localio, A. Russell and eight other authors. "Relation Between Malpractice Claims and Adverse Events Due to Negligence: Results of the Harvard Medical Practice Study III." *New England Journal of Medicine 325:*245–51, 1991. **p. 15:** "In Sweden…the mechanism for compensating patients": Rosenthal, Marilynn. *Dealing with Medical Malpractice—The British and Swedish Experience.* London and Durham, N.C.: Tavistock and Duke University Press, 1988. **p. 16:** "Overtreatment of the insured": Franks, Peter, Clancy, Carolyn M., and Nutting, Paul A. "Gatekeeping Revisited—Protecting Patients from Overtreatment." *New England Journal of Medicine 327:*424–9, 1992. **p. 16:** "the well known uninsured population": Friedman, Emily. "The Uninsured: From Dilemma to Crisis." *Journal of the American Medical Association 265:*2491–5, 1991; part of a special issue of the journal devoted to "Caring for the Uninsured and Underinsured." **p. 16:** " 'cherry picking' ": Freudenheim, Milt. "Insurers Accused of Discrimination in AIDS Coverage." *New York Times,* June 1, 1993. **p. 17:** " 'policy churning' ": Kolata, Gina. "New Insurance Practice: Dividing Sick from Well." *New York Times,* March 4, 1992, p. A1. **p. 17:** "*four times as fast* as the number of doctors": Weissman, Gerald. *The Doctor Dilemma: Squaring the Old Values With the New Economy.* Knoxville, Tenn.: Whittle Books, The Grand Rounds Press, 1992.

p. 17: "the cost of this harassment in the morale of physicians": Astrachan, Anthony and Weissman, Gerald. "The Hassle Factor." Series of six articles in *MD* magazine, May–December 1991. Based on a survey of 1700 physicians. See also Belkin, Lisa. "Sensing a Loss of Control, More Doctors Call It Quits," *New York Times*, March 9, 1993, and her "Doctors Lose Autonomy to Health-Care Networks," ibid., November 12, 1991. **p. 18:** "no longer just the poor": This discussion is based on Eckholm, Erik. "The Uninsured: 37 Million and Growing." *New York Times*, "News of the Week," Sunday, July 11, 1993. **p. 20:** "What scams?": Quinn, Jane Bryant. "Insurance: The Death Spiral." *Newsweek*, February 2, 1993, p. 47. **p. 20:** "A representative of Consumers Union": Pear, Robert. "Insurers Facing Closer Scrutiny in Clinton Plan." *New York Times*, June 22, 1993, p. A1. **p. 21:** "inflation that makes health care costs soar": Schieber, George J., Poullier, Jean-Pierre, and Greenwald, Leslie M. "Health Care Systems in Twenty-Four Countries." *Health Affairs* 10:22–38, 1991. **p. 22:** "a vast, parasitic, private corporate bureaucracy": Woolhandler, Steffie, and Himmelstein, David. "The Deteriorating Administrative Efficiency of the U.S. Health Care System." *New England Journal of Medicine* 324:1253–8, 1991. **p. 22:** "Most recently...Dr. Steffie Woolhandler": Woolhandler, S., Himmelstein, David U., and Lewontin, James P. *New England Journal of Medicine* 329:400–3, 1993. **p. 22:** "Moving aggressively into managed care itself": Kerr, Peter. "The Changing Definition of Health Insurers." *New York Times*, May 10, 1991, p. C1. **p. 23:** " 'private insurance is big business in America' ": Inglehart, John. "The American Health Care System: Private Insurance." *New England Journal of Medicine* 326: 1715–20, 1992, p. 1716.

p. 23: "The slide continued, and continues": Stimmel, Barry. "The Crisis in Primary Care and the Role of Medical Schools: Defining the Issues." *Journal of the American Medical Association* 268:2060–5, 1992. **p. 23:** "An analysis published in 1993": Mullan, Fitzhugh, Rivo, Marc L., and Politzer, Robert M. "Doctors, Dollars, and Determination: Making Physician Work–Force Policy." *Health Affairs* 12 (Supplement):138–51, 1993. **p. 25:** "according to Governor Howard Dean": Interviewed at the National Governors' Association convention, Tulsa, Oklahoma, August 16, 1993, C-SPAN. **p. 25:** "A 1989 study": Shulkin, D.J. "Choice of Specialty: It's Money that Matters in the USA." *Journal of the American Medical Association* 262:1630, 1989. **p. 25:** "Surgeons and other specialists took...advantage": Starr, Paul. *The Social Transformation of American Medicine*. New York: Basic Books, 1982, pp. 347–63. **pp. 25–26:** " 'The currency of primary care is time' ": Hart, Julian Tudor. "Two Paths for Medical Practice." *Lancet* 340:772–5, September 26, 1992. **p. 26:** "Studies of compliance": Carr, John E., and Maxim, Peter E. "Communication Research and the Doctor-Patient Relationship." In John E. Carr and Harold A. Dengerink, eds. *Behavioral Science in the Practice of Medicine*. New York: Elsevier, 1983, pp. 152–61. See also Kessler, David A. "Communicating With Patients About Their Medications." *New England Journal of Medicine* 325:1650–2, 1991. **p. 27:** "medical scientists like John Wennberg": Wennberg, John and Gittelsohn, Alan. "Variation in Medical Care Among Small Areas." *Scientific American* 246:120–34, 1982. **p. 27:** "David Eddy of Duke University": Eddy, David M. "Clinical Decision Making: From Theory to Practice." *Journal of the American Medical Association* 263:287–90, 1990; ibid., 441–3; ibid., 877–80; ibid., 1265–75; ibid., 1839–41; ibid., 2239–43; ibid., 2493–2505; ibid., 3077–3084; vol. 264:389–91, 1990; ibid., 1161–70; ibid., 1737–9; vol. 265:105–8, 1991; ibid., 782–8; ibid., 1446–50; ibid. 2399–2404; vol. 266:417–20, 1991; ibid., 2135–41; ibid., 2439–45. **p. 28:** "studies of the tonsillectomy fad": Wennberg, John E., Blowers, Lewis, Parker, Robert, and Gittelsohn, Alan M. "Changes in Tonsillectomy Rates Associated With Feedback and Review." *Pediatrics* 59:821–6, 1977.

p. 28: "A brain bypass operation": The EC/IC Bypass Group. "Failure of Extracranial-Intracranial Arterial Bypass to Reduce the Risk of Ischemic Stroke: Results of an International Randomized Trial." *New England Journal of Medicine* 313:1191–1200, 1985; and follow-up article with reply to critics, 316:817–824. **p. 29:** "Unwarranted hysterectomies": Carlson, Karen J., Nichols, David H., and Schiff, Isaac. "Indications for hysterectomy." *New England Journal of Medicine* 328:856–60, 1993. **p. 29:** "Contrast this with...Saskatchewan": Dyck, Frank J., and ten other authors. "Effect of Surveillance on the Number of Hysterectomies in the Province of Saskatchewan." *New England Journal of Medicine* 296:1326–8, 1977. **p. 29:** "A runaway prostate surgery fad": Fleming, Craig, Wasson, John H., Albertsen, Peter C., Barry, Michael J., and Wennberg, John E. "A Decision Analysis of Alternative Treatment Strategies for Clinically Localized Prostate Cancer." *Journal of the American Medical Association* 269:2650–8, 1993; with accompanying editorial.

p. 30: "How about pacemaker implantation?": Greenspan, Allan M., and five other authors. "Incidence of Unwarranted Implantation of Permanent Cardiac Pacemakers in a Large Medical Population." *New England Journal of Medicine 318*:158–63, 1988.   **p. 30:** "Or…carotid endarterectomy": Committee on Health Care Issues, American Neurological Association. "Does Carotid Endarterectomy Decrease Stroke and Death in Patients with Transient Ischemic Attacks?" *Annals of Neurology 22*:72–6, 1987.   **p. 31:** "Look at coronary angiograms": Chassin, Mark R., Kosecoff, Jacqueline, Solomon, David H., and Brook, Robert H. "How Coronary Angiography is Used: Clinical Determinants of Appropriateness." *Journal of the American Medical Association 258*:2543–7, 1987.   **p. 31:** "you are getting unneeded treatments": Black, William C., and Welch, Gilbert. "Advances in Diagnostic Imaging and Overestimations of Disease Prevalence and the Benefits of Therapy." *New England Journal of Medicine 328*:1237–41, 1993. Bell, Bertram. "New Medical Technology Could Do You Harm." Letter, *New York Times,* June 1, 1993.   **p. 32:** "Franklin Yee": Altman, Lawrence K. "How Tools of Medicine Can Get in the Way." *New York Times,* May 12, 1992.   **p. 32:** "the old Reagan-Bush bromide": For example, Dr. Louis Sullivan, Secretary of Health and Human Services, stated that "the United States health care system is the most advanced in the world." MacNeil/Lehrer Newshour, January 15, 1992. Transcript by Strictly Business, Overland Park, Kansas.   **p. 33:** "The Clinton version": Speech to the National Governors' Association, Tulsa, Oklahoma, August 16, 1993.   **p. 33:** "excess mortality in Harlem": McCord, Colin, and Freeman, Harold. "Excess Mortality in Harlem." *New England Journal of Medicine 322*:173–7, 1990.   **p. 35:** "A 1991 study in East Baltimore": Sommer, Alfred, and nine others. "Racial Differences in the Cause-Specific Prevalence of Blindness in East Baltimore." *New England Journal of Medicine 325*:1412–22, 1991; editorial by Johanna M. Seddon, pp. 1440–2.

p. 36: "uninsured and Medicaid patients have much higher rates": Weissman, Joel S., Gatsonis, Constantine, and Epstein, Arnold M. "Rates of Avoidable Hospitalization by Insurance Status in Massachusetts and Maryland." *Journal of the American Medical Association 268*:2388–94, 1992.   **p. 36:** "turned away from or out of American hospitals": Annas, George J. "Your Money or Your Life: 'Dumping' Uninsured Patients from Hospital Emergency Wards." *American Journal of Public Health 76*:74–7, 1986. For a dramatic account of recent consequences in one state, see Perl, Rebecca. " 'Patient Dumping': Law Doing Little to End Hospital Practice." *Atlanta Journal-Constitution,* September 29, 1991, p. 1.   **p. 37:** "4,675 women…who had invasive breast cancer": Ayanian, John Z., Kohler, Betsy A., Abe, Toshi, and Epstein, Arnold M. "The Relation Between Health Insurance Coverage and Clinical Outcomes Among Women With Breast Cancer." *New England Journal of Medicine 329*:326–31, 1993.   **p. 37:** "A 1992 study in New York State": Burstin, Helen R., Lipsitz, Stuart R., and Brennan, Troyen A. "Socioeconomic Status and Risk for Substandard Medical Care." *Journal of the American Medical Association 268*:2383–7; with accompanying editorial by Bindman, Andrew B., and Grumbach, Kevin. "America's Safety Net: The Wrong Place at the Wrong Time?," pp. 2426–7.   **p. 38:** "if you want an inoculation": Rosenthal, Elisabeth. "Hurdle for Preventive Medicine: Insurance." *New York Times,* April 19, 1990.

The Cause

p. 41: "the first great *social* transformation": Starr, Paul. *The Social Transformation of American Medicine.* New York: Basic Books, 1982.   **p. 42:** "In 1937, health reform was…front page news": As reviewed by Beeson, Paul. "An Early Call for Health Care Reform: The Committee of 430 Physicians." *The Pharos,* Winter 1993, pp. 22–4.   **p. 43:** "Dr. Morris Fishbein…must go down in history": Beeson, work cited, and Meyer, Karl E. " 'Socialized Medicine' Revisited: How Doctors Doomed Truman's Health Plan." *New York Times,* August 2, 1993, Editorials/ Letters page.   **p. 44:** "Harry Truman's original proposal": This discussion relies heavily on Starr, Paul. *The Social Transformation of American Medicine,* pp. 235–334. The comparative international history of health reform in the postwar period can be found in Starr, Paul, and Immergut, Ellen, "Health Care and the Boundaries of Politics." In Maier, Charles S., ed., *Changing Boundaries of the Political.* Cambridge: Cambridge University Press, 1986.   **p. 44:** "In Canada, the evolution of universal care": Taylor, Malcolm G. *Insuring National Health Care: The Canadian Experience.* Chapel Hill, N.C.: University of North Carolina Press, 1990.   **p. 45:** "Meanwhile, back in the U.S.A.": Starr, *Social Transformation,* ibid. Events are as Starr recounts them, but some of the interpretation and emphasis is mine.   **p. 48:** "The great beneficiaries…of the seventies": Starr, pp. 335–449.

p. 48: "a 1980 article in *Fortune*": as cited by Starr, p. 436.   **p. 48:** "Relman…introduced the term 'medical-industrial complex' ": Relman, Arnold S. "The New Medical-Industrial Complex." *New England Journal of Medicine 303*:963–70, 1980.   **p. 50:** "Insurance companies were gobbling up HMOs": Kerr, Peter. "The Changing Definition of Health Insurers." *New York Times*, May 10, 1991, p. C1.   **p. 50:** " 'I envision the insurance companies transforming themselves into HMOs…' ": Kenneth S. Abramowitz, of Sanford C. Bernstein, quoted in Kerr, ibid., p. C2.   **p. 50:** " 'a bet-the-company drive…' ": Kerr, Peter. "Betting the Farm on Managed Care." *New York Times*, June 27, 1993, Section 3, p. 1.   **p. 52:** "almost $300 billion…controlled by corporate sources": Inglehart, John. "The American Health Care System: Private Insurance." *New England Journal of Medicine 326*: 1715–20, 1992, p. 1717, Table 1, for the national figures here.   **p. 53:** "The 1991 salaries of the top executives": Hilts, Philip J. "Doctors' Pay Resented, and It's Underestimated." *New York Times*, March 31, 1993, p. A9.   **p. 53:** "Only a small minority…commit outright fraud": Witkin, Gordon, with Dorian Friedman and Monika Guttman. "Health Care Fraud." *U.S. News and World Report*, February 24, 1992.   **p. 53:** "invest in facilities to which they then refer": Inglehart, John. "Efforts to Address the Problem of Physician Self-Referral." *New England Journal of Medicine 325*:1820–4, 1992. See also Meier, Barry. "Doctors' Investments in Home Care Grow, Raising Fears of Ethical Swamp." *New York Times*, March 19, 1993, p. A10.

p. 54: "In 1992…a profit margin of 13 percent": Drake, Donald, and Uhlman, Marian. *Making Medicine, Making Money.* Kansas City, Mo.: Andrews and McMeel, 1993. Originally a five-part series in *Philadelphia Enquirer.*   **p. 54:** "Top executives in six leading companies": Hilts, Philip J., as cited above.   **p. 54:** "their claims about research": Rosenthal, Elisabeth. "Exploring the Murky World of Drug Prices." *New York Times*, March 28, 1992, News of the Week in Review. See also her "Drug Companies' Profits Finance More Promotion than Research," ibid., February 21, 1993, p. 1, and Hilts, Philip, "U.S. Study of Drug Makers Criticizes 'Excess Profits'," ibid., February 26, 1993, p. C1.   **p. 54:** "104 of the 287 most frequently prescribed drugs": Wolfe, Sidney M., Fugate, Lisa, Hulstrand, Elizabeth P., Kamimoto, Laurie E., and others. *Worst Pills, Best Pills: The Older Adult's Guide to Avoiding Drug-Induced Death or Illness.* Washington, D.C.: Public Citizen Health Research Group, 1988.   **p. 54:** "high-pressure sales techniques": Chren, Mary-Margaret, Landefeld, Seth, and Murray, Thomas H. "Doctors, Drug Companies, and Gifts." *Journal of the American Medical Association 262*:3448–51, 1989.   **p. 54:** "a major factor in health care waste": Rosenthal, Elisabeth. "As Costs of New Drugs Rise, Hospitals Stick by Old Ones." *New York Times*, December 18, 1991, p. A1.   **p. 54:** "experts…reviewed 109 full-page drug ads": Wilkes, Michael S., Doblin, Bruce H., and Shapiro, Martin F. "Pharmaceutical Advertisements in Leading Medical Journals: Experts' Assessments." *Annals of Internal Medicine 116*:912–9, 1992; with accompanying editorials by David A. Kessler and by Robert and Suzanne Fletcher.   **p. 55:** "no way for the FDA to monitor all of them": Kessler, David A. "Drug Promotion and Scientific Exchange: The Role of the Clinical Investigator." *New England Journal of Medicine 325*:201–3, 1991.   **p. 55:** "network of illegal pharmacies": Kolata, Gina. "Patients Turning to Illegal Pharmacies." *New York Times*, November 4, 1991, p. A1.   **p. 55:** "Joseph Califano…estimated": Califano, Joseph. "The Best Hope." *Health Management Quarterly*, April 1991, Vol. 13, #2, pp. 24–6.

p. 56: "Warren E. Burger…wrote in 1991": Burger, Warren E. "Too Many Lawyers, Too Many Suits." Review of *The Litigation Explosion*, by Walter K. Olson. *New York Times Book Review*, May 12, 1991, p. 12.   **p. 56:** "What *Forbes*…calls 'the tort tax' ": Spencer, Leslie. "The Tort Tax." *Forbes*, February 17, 1992, pp. 40–2.   **p. 56:** "cesaren section…likely where malpractice claims are high": Localio, A. Russell, and six other authors. "Relationship Between Malpractice Claims and Cesarean Delivery." *Journal of the American Medical Association 269*:366–73, 1993.   **p. 57:** "thirty times as many lawsuits as Japan": This and other statistics that follow are from Gergen, David. "America's Legal Mess." *U.S. News and World Report*, August 19, 1991, p. 72.   **p. 57:** "Sweden has a no-fault system": Rosenthal, Marilynn. *Dealing with Medical Malpractice—The British and Swedish Experience.* London and Durham, N.C.: Tavistock and Duke University Press, 1988.   **p. 57:** "No-fault insurance works.": Manuel, Barry M. "Professional Liability—A No-Fault Solution." *New England Journal of Medicine 322*:627–31, 1990; with accompanying editorial by Arnold S. Relman, pp. 626–7.   **p. 59:** "the *New York Times* has been much less fair": Bauduy, Jennifer. "Missing the Beat: *The New York Times* and America's Health Care Crisis." Thesis submitted to the Columbia University School of Journalism in partial fulfillment of the requirements for the Master's degree, 1994.

p. 59: "Four members of its board of directors": Sulzberger, Arthur Ochs. "Notice of 1993 Annual Meeting and Proxy Statement." The New York Times Company, 229 West 43rd Street, New York, New York, 10036.   **p. 59:** "two Democratic senators deeply involved in health reform": Bycel, Benjamin. "Doing the Health-Care Hustle." *New York Times*, July 21, 1993, Op-Ed page.   **p. 59:** " 'the people who yelled the loudest' ": Toner, Robin. "Health Care Plan Moves to Center of Political Stage." *New York Times,* August 9, 1993, pp. A1/A8.   **p. 60:** "pump enormous amounts of cash": Mollison, Andrew. "Health Industry Pumps Cash Into Campaigns." *Atlanta Journal-Constitution*, April 4, 1993.   **p. 60:** "One lobbyist…told *Newsweek*": Waldman, Steven, and Cohn, Bob. "Health-Lobby Mania." *Newsweek*, July 5, 1993, pp. 38–40.   **p. 60:** "slickly produced…ad campaigns": Kurtz, Howard. "For Health Care Lobbies, a Major Ad Operation." *Washington Post*, April 13, 1993, and ads seen in various newspapers and magazines, spring and summer 1993.   **p. 62:** "a 76-year-old woman got a liver transplant": de Lissovoy, Gregory. "Medicare and Heart Transplants: Will Lightning Strike Twice?" *Health Affairs* 7:61–72, 1988.   **p. 62:** "articles…in leading medical journals": Edmunds, L. Henry, et al. "Open-Heart Surgery in Octogenarians." *New England Journal of Medicine 319*:131–6, 1988; Hosking, Michael, et al. "Outcomes of Surgery in Patients 90 Years of Age and Older." *Journal of the American Medical Association 261*:1909–15, 1989.   **p. 62:** "limits have to be set": Callahan, Daniel. *Setting Limits: Medical Goals in an Aging Society*. New York: Simon and Schuster, 1987. See also Callahan, Daniel. "Why We Must Set Limits." In Homer, Paul and Holstein, Martha, eds. *A Good Old Age?: The Paradox of Setting Limits*. New York: Simon and Schuster, 1990, p. 23. (This book collects articles in the debate on Callahan's radical proposal.) Oregon has pioneered such limits. See Eddy, David M. "Oregon's Plan: Should It Be Approved?" *Journal of the American Medical Association 266*:2439–45, 1991; Steinbrook, Robert, and Lo, Bernard. "The Oregon Medicaid Demonstration Project—Will It Provide Adequate Medical Care?" *New England Journal of Medicine 326*:340–4, 1992.

THE CURE

p. 66: "patients in these plans are very dissatisfied": Freudenheim, Milt. "Many Patients Unhappy With H.M.O.'s." *New York Times*, August 18, 1993.   **p. 67:** " 'It's the dark side of managed care.' ": ibid.   **p. 67:** " 'lured, or kicked, into a health maintenance organization' ": Quinn, Jane Bryant. "Forcing You Into an HMO." *Newsweek*, September 12, 1988.   **p. 69:** "McNamara…invented the term 'managed competition' ": The attribution of this claim to Shapley may be found in Yamin, Priscilla, and Dreyfuss, Robert. "The Godfather of Managed Competition." *Mother Jones*, May/June 1993, p. 20. The thoroughly top-down nature of McNamara's management theory and practice (learned by Enthoven at McNamara's knee) is evident in her biography: Shapley, Deborah. *Promise and Power: The Life and Times of Robert McNamara*. Boston: Little, Brown, 1993.   **p. 69:** "the 'Whiz Kids'…unsurpassed intellectual arrogance": Trewbitt, Henry L. *McNamara*. New York: Harper & Row, 1971, p. 12ff.   **p. 69:** "faced down a group of white-haired generals": ibid., p. 13.   **p. 69:** " 'What's missing is the essence…judgment…' ": General Davis is quoted in Nolan, Janne E. *Guardians of the Arsenal: The Politics of Nuclear Strategy*. New York: Basic Books, 1989, p. 69.   **p. 70:** "benefits package would not cover vision care": Hubner, John. "The Abandoned Father of Health-Care Reform." *New York Times Magazine*, July 18, 1993.

p. 70: "this would abandon almost every person": Brodie, Scott E. "Health-Care Reform." Letter. *New York Times Magazine*, August 8, 1993, p. 10.   **p. 70:** "the Jackson Hole, Wyoming ski resort": This account is based on Hubner, and on Yamin and Dreyfuss, as cited above. **p. 71:** "no consumer, labor, or senior citizen groups": Ellwood, P.M, Enthoven, A.C., and Etheredge, L. "The Jackson Hole Initiatives for a Twenty-First Century American Health Care System." *Health Economics* 1:149–168, 1992.   **p. 71:** "a director and stockholder of PCS, Inc.": Yamin and Dreyfuss, as cited above.   **p. 71:** "Ira Magaziner, the official head of President Clinton's Task Force on National Health Care Reform": For the account of his career, see Pear, Robert. "An Idealist's New Task: To Revamp Health Care." *New York Times*, February 26, 1993.   **p. 73:** "Mrs. Clinton…a very talented lawyer": See Warner, Judith. *Hillary Clinton: The Inside Story*, New York: Signet, 1993, for a positive account of her life and achievements. **p. 74:** "to try to conduct…health reform in secret": Clift, Eleanor, and Hager, Mary. "Health Care: Covert Operation." *Newsweek*, March 15, 1993.   **p. 74:** "Interested parties…had to take the White House to court": Pear, Robert. "Court Questions Job Status of Hillary Clinton on Panel," *New York Times*, May 1, 1993; and his "Court Rules That the First Lady Is a 'De Facto' Federal Official." ibid., June 23, 1993.

p. 74: "a self-assured moral crusader": Kelly, Michael. "Saint Hillary." *New York Times Magazine*, May 23, 1993. **p. 75:** " 'I want to be a voice for children…' ": Warner, p. 8. **p. 76:** "a consistent air of bumbling and waffling": Friedman, Thomas L. "Clinton Rules Out Delay In Unveiling Health-Care Plan." *New York Times*, April 28, 1993. **p. 77:** "tradition of vagueness": Editorial, "Ambiguous Salvo On Health Care." *New York Times*, August 18, 1993. **p. 78:** "Nader has joked": Nader, Ralph, addressing *Health Care Reform Week*'s conference, "President Clinton's Health Care Reforms," June 14, 1993. **p. 79:** "Clinton says five to seven years": In his August 16, 1993, speech to the Governors. **p. 79:** "a leading advocate of a Canadian-style plan": Woolhandler, Steffie. "Why Not Simplify Health Reform?" *USA Today*, June 24, 1993, p. 13A. **p. 79:** "Mrs. Clinton's strategy…declare war on doctors": Passell, Peter. "The Dangers of Declaring War on Doctors." *New York Times*, March 21, 1993. **p. 81:** "The dominant advisers in the task force": Toner, Robin. "Hillary Clinton's Potent Brain Trust On Health Reform." *New York Times*, February 28, 1993, Section 3, p. 1. **p. 81:** "According to John Motley": Addressing the National Governors' Association convention, Tulsa, Oklahoma, August 16, 1993.

p. 81: "Early retirees aged fifty-five to sixty-five": Priest, Dana. "Health Care Reform Plan to Propose Federal Coverage for Early Retirees." *Washington Post*, September 7, 1993, p. A6. See also Freudenheim, Milt. "Health Limbo for Early Retirees." *New York Times*, July 10, 1993. **pp. 81–82:** "No one…claims that managed competition could…work in rural America": Kronick, Richard, Goodman, David C., Wennberg, John, and Wagner, Edward. "The Marketplace In Health Care Reform: The Demographic Limitations of Managed Competition." *New England Journal of Medicine 328*:148–52, 1993, with accompanying editorial by Arnold S. Relman. **p. 82:** "there is a solution…in Congress": Wellstone, Paul (D-MN). "The American Health Security Act of 1993," S. 491. Introduced March 3, 1993. The proposal is explained further in Wellstone, Paul D., and Shaffer, Ellen R. "The American Health Security Act: A Single-Payer Proposal." *New England Journal of Medicine 328*:1489–93, 1993. **p. 86:** "Misconceptions and outright lies…a virtual disinformation campaign": For the truth about health care delivery and medicine in Canada, see Taylor, Malcolm G. *Insuring National Health Care: The Canadian Experience*, Chapel Hill, N.C.: University of North Carolina, 1990, and our own government's report, "Canadian Health Insurance: Lessons for the United States," General Accounting Office/HRD-91-90, June 1991. See also Evans, Robert G., and ten other authors. "Controlling Health Expenditures—The Canadian Reality." *New England Journal of Medicine 320*:571–7, 1989; and Fuchs, Victor R. and Hahn, James S. "How Does Canada Do It?: A Comparison of Expenditures for Physicians' Services in the United States and Canada." ibid., vol. *323*:884–90, 1990.

p. 88: "Canadians doctors…rated the quality of care": *Physician's Management,* August 1992. **p. 88:** "Canadian doctors have higher levels of satisfaction": Blendon, Robert J., and nine other authors. "Physicians' Perspectives on Caring for Patients in the United States, Canada, and West Germany." *New England Journal of Medicine 328*:1011–16, 1993. **p. 88:** "an additional $100 to $150 billion": Pear, Robert. "Health-Care Costs May Be Increased $100 Billion a Year." *New York Times*, May 3, 1993. **p. 89:** "questions whether the plan will work to control costs at all": Congressional Budget Office. "Managed Competition and Its Potential to Reduce Health Spending." Congress of the United States, May 1993. **p. 89:** "four serious estimates…under a single payer": Congressional Budget Office. "Single Payer and All-Payer Health Insurance Systems Using Medicare's Payment Rates." CBO Staff Memorandum. Congress of the United States, April 1993. **p. 90:** "all these countries…have health care delivery superior to ours": Saltman, Richard B. "Single-Source Financing Systems: A Solution for the United States?" *Journal of the American Medical Association 268*:774–9, 1992. See also Saltman, Richard B. and Von Otter, Casten. *Planned Markets and Public Competition: Strategic Reform in Northern European Health Systems.* Buckingham, Eng.: Open University Press, 1993.

Acknowledgments

THIS BOOK OWES MUCH to my editor, Nancy Miller, who believed it was possible to produce it within a few months. Mark Corsey, Meg Fry, Pat Jalbert, and my agent, Elaine Markson, were also crucial to the process.

Dr. Henry Kahn first taught me about the need for a single payer; Dr. Ronald Barr about the Canadian system; Professor Richard Saltman, other national health care systems; Ellen Shaffer, the Wellstone bill; Dr. Julian Tudor Hart, the role of primary care; Dr. Wyche Stubbs, the viewpoint of the medical director of a large American hospital; David Levine, that of a CEO of a large Canadian one. Martin Freeth, Stefan Moore, and Jane West taught me much about the health care crisis in international perspective. Professor James Gustafson helped me to think through the ethical questions, and Dr. S. Boyd Eaton presented the viewpoint of physicians who fear government interference.

Others who shared their expertise include Doctors John Stone, Herbert Karp, Ira Schwartz, William Foege, Ian MacColl, Steven Cohen-Cole, David Eddy, Arthur Kleinman, Philip Savitsky, Neil Shulman, Sally McNagny, Margaret Mermin, Andre Nahmias, Stuart Seidman, Charles Wickliffe, Timothy Harlan, Richard Leff, Perry Brickman, and Jennifer Weil; and Professors Carol Worthman, Wenda Trevathan, Ronda Stavisky, Robert Hahn, Arthur Shostak, Fred Kroger, and Paul Starr. The manuscript was read by Dr. Julian Gomez and Professor Peter Brown. Neither they nor anyone else but me bears any responsibility for my opinions or my errors.

Kathy Mote provided every variety of support and friendship. Research assistance was provided by Nancy Lee, Martha Dameron, Michele Renay, Kate Ackerman, and Catherine Drew. I thank too the Department of Anthropology and the administration of Emory University, particularly Professor Peggy Barlett, President James T. Laney, and Provost William Frye.

Early influences on my idea of what a doctor should be included Milton Finkel, Abraham ("Bobby") Fink, Leon Fink, and Martin Silbersweig—all dedicated primary care doctors. Teachers who guided my medical education include Doctors Paul Pavel, Stefan Stein, Hans Bode, Joseph Lipinski, Walter Abelmann, T. Berry Brazelton, Norman Geschwind, Daniel Federman, Edward Gross, Ross Neisuler, H. Thomas Ballantine, David Hamburg, Francis Moore, and Leon Eisenberg. Doctors John Stone, Herbert Karp, Boyd Eaton, Julian Gomez, and Ira Schwartz have been influential models, as well as friends, in the time since.

Betty Castellani made this book possible by insisting that life must go on in the face of illness. Robert Leibman, Joseph Beck, Irven DeVore, and Herbert Perluck have been valued advisers and friends. Ronnie Wenker Konner, Hannah Konner, and Irving Konner shared their experience of illness. My brother, Larry Konner, is also my closest friend; we have weathered many trials together. The same is true of my wife, Marjorie Shostak; her support for my work on this book during a difficult time in her own life has been crucial indeed. Finally, my children, Susanna, Adam, and Sarah, now understand what goes into making a book and what my preoccupation with it may have cost them. Their generosity has been real, and I am grateful.